Dictionary of
English Antique Furniture

for
Rosalind

Douglas Ash

Dictionary of
English Antique Furniture

FREDERICK MULLER

First published in Great Britain 1970
by Frederick Muller Ltd., Fleet Street, London, E.C.4

Printed and bound by The Garden City Press Limited
Letchworth, Hertfordshire
SBN: 584 10060 4

Introduction

There are many excellent books about traditional English furniture, some of them being mentioned in the Bibliography, but the necessary shortness of the list should not be taken as derogatory to those which are not included. The purpose of this Dictionary is to provide reference material in a more easily accessible form and to furnish basic information for those who are attracted to the subject, but have not yet had an opportunity to study it in depth.

Its depth is, in fact, almost limitless, for in this, as in other branches of art-history, there is always something more to learn; but far from being a cause of frustration this is one of its most fascinating aspects.

The applied arts may be considered as part of the social history of a nation; but since each generation is largely indifferent to the achievements of that which preceded it and, in fact, tends deliberately to turn its back upon them in order to establish its own identity, history only yields its secrets slowly and painfully as a result of devoted research. This is no doubt partly the reason why myth is often allowed to masquerade as fact in the many circumstances in which full information is not yet available, and misleading jargon terms gain an acceptance which should be denied to them, for it is better to admit to ignorance than to tamper with the truth. On the other hand, narrow pedantry is always to be avoided as far as possible, for if a language is to remain alive it must be prepared to absorb new words which express, in ellipsis, what could previously be expressed only in lengthy phrases. An example of this is furnished by the word 'tallboy'. But purely capricious terms, which take the place of satisfactory existing ones with sound ancestry, should always be rejected, not only because they tend to destroy our language but also because they make a subject which is already complicated enough even more difficult, by erecting artificial barriers between us and the past.

Some of these terms, such as 'cock-fighting chair' (a thing which never existed) and 'tea poy' (which owes its corrupt significance to popular ignorance in the mid-19th century) are discussed in the following pages; but as no ordinary dictionary can set out to be a dictionary of incorrect terms there are doubtless many omissions. This need not, however, cause any particular despondency.

Some readers may have acquired certain misconceptions through contact with less well-informed sections of the antiques trade, but it is nevertheless entirely necessary that academic study should be reinforced by practical experience. This may be gained from museums, auction-rooms of the better sort and shops, the last two having the advantage that items of furniture may be handled and examined. The question of Reproductions is dealt with briefly in a special section following this Introduction.

Why are people attracted to antique furniture? Whether one likes it or not, nearly all that is beautiful in the British heritage is due to the Church and the old aristocracy, but the fact remains that this heritage is for everyone, not just a few experts. No one need be afraid of a subject which is as much part of their history as anyone else's. Every piece of wooden furniture ever made was once part of a tree, and even the most inexperienced beginner can, by imagining the worthy craftsmen of past ages chiselling, carving, polishing and so forth, bring to the most sophisticated object some degree of comprehension and appreciation. The attraction is probably partly romantic, partly due to a reaction against the machine-age in which our world seems to become constantly uglier and in which the human spirit becomes increasingly downgraded, so that many people, casting about in bewilderment for some sense of purpose, are even reduced to worshipping motorcars. Into something which is largely hand-made the maker inevitably injects part of his own personality, and this results in there being something of humanity present even in a piece of shaped wood. This is subtly reassuring and imparts a comforting sense of continuity and the inherent dignity of man.

Apart from emotional and aesthetic factors, a study of the history of furniture gives us criteria of judgment upon which assessments of later manufactures can be based, for it is not enough that something should be merely different from what has gone before: it should be as good or better. With the passage of time, the task of designers in search of originality becomes increasingly hopeless and they are deserving of our sympathy, but this does not mean that we are obliged to accept all their productions with adulation or complacency. The author once saw the design of an oblong dining-table with square-section iron legs described as 'brilliant', but a recollection of the great styles of the past made this conception seem not only paltry but even insolent.

If used properly, this book will lead the enquiring reader down all kinds of fascinating by-roads. If he undertakes these excursions with willingness and enthusiasm they will enrich his life and ensure that his tastes and opinions are based on something more solid than tendentious journalism or television advertisements.

ACKNOWLEDGEMENTS

The author wishes to thank Lady Muriel Martin and Mrs. Beatrice Haswell who kindly read the proofs.

Reproductions

Reproductions of furniture in earlier styles began to be made just before the Victorian period, especially in the form of florid chairs with twist-turning and other elements of a vaguely 17th-century character. These owed their introduction to the romantic atmosphere engendered by Sir Walter Scott's historical novels, but they were not accurate copies and could not deceive anyone acquainted with the originals from which they ostensibly derived.

Fairly modern reproductions of 17th-century oak pieces such as press cupboards are also unconvincing, owing to the difficulty of simulating the patine of true age, unless they have been deliberately assembled from parts of genuinely antique objects; but even these arouse suspicion after a careful examination which discloses such inconsistencies as dribbles of glue, new pegs, hinges attached by screws and evidence of the use of stain.

The chief danger stems from items in mahogany which are in the styles current from about 1750 to 1800. If they are modern they usually present little difficulty, as parts from which French polish has been worn off by normal rubbing show wood of a very light tone. In the Georgian period, mahogany was seasoned by steeping it in water for many years and this caused it to turn red throughout its substance, but as present-day economic conditions would make such treatment unprofitable, the timber remains almost white beneath the polish on the surface. In connection with French polish it might be mentioned that although this was not used in England before the second quarter of the 19th century, it was sometimes applied later to genuine 18th-century objects which had been neglected, in order to give them a fresh and bright appearance. If, however, there is evidence that the timber was never treated in any other manner the piece is un-doubtedly a reproduction.

Some Victorian reproductions have by now a considerable amount of age which has conferred upon them a very respectable appearance of antiquity, and when 18th-century designs have been faithfully copied, reproductions are sometimes almost impossible to distinguish from originals.

This is particularly true in regard to plain tripod tables. Examples with carved ornament seldom pose any problems which survive investigation, but plain specimens often provide little or no outward evidence upon which a definite opinion may be based. Such tables almost invariably have tip-up tops, and these should be carefully examined for signs of wear in the pivots and the holes in which they work. These parts in Georgian originals have often had twice the amount of use as their later counterparts, and this has frequently caused the pivot almost to wear through one side of the hole and brought about a noticeable looseness between the block which surmounts the pillar and the underside of the top. Some people comfort themselves with the notion that the type of tripod table with a 'bird-cage' beneath the top—that is, a square platform connected to the block by four small, turned columns—was never made in the Victorian era, but this, unfortunately, is an illusion.

Reputable dealers in antiquities whose opinions are based not only on years of experience but also on a scholarly interest in the subject will give a written guarantee of authenticity if required. The secondhand furniture trade is, however, somewhat overcrowded, and all dealers do not necessarily fit wholly into the above category, largely on account of a tendency to believe what they wish to believe. This weakness is especially apparent in relation to the numerous bow-fronted chests of drawers made in the Victorian period in imitation of those of the last quarter of the 18th century.

Nineteenth-century reproductions are often equipped with the large, wooden mushroom-shaped handles common at the time, and the tendentious suggestion is sometimes made that these were applied in replacement of 18th-century brass handles to bring the piece up to date.

This suggestion should always be received with suspicion, more especially if the chest concerned is over 3 ft. 6 in. high, and its validity can often be tested by an examination of the front and inside of the drawer, bearing in mind the following facts about late-18th-century handles. These were of three types only on normal chests of drawers: (*a*) a loop-shaped drop-handle pivoted at each end from a pierced knob forming the head of a threaded bolt which passed *via* a brass disc through the thickness of the drawer and was secured by a circular brass nut on the inside; (*b*) a similar handle backed by a large oval escutcheon plate; (*c*) a ring-handle suspended from a small loop at the top of a circular brass escutcheon plate, the loop forming the head of a single bolt with a nut on the inside of the drawer.

If the wooden mushroom-shaped handle has replaced type (*a*) there should either be traces of the original two holes for the bolts on the outside and inside of the drawer, or noticeable evidence of their having been plugged; the same applies to type (*b*), with the additional likelihood of the edges of the oval plate having marked the surface of the wood. The situation is a little more complicated if the original handles were of type (*c*), as there would originally have been only one hole for each single bolt, and this could have been enlarged to accommodate the thick, threaded wooden shank of the Victorian mushroom. Even in this case, however, certain facts can be of assistance. First, the centre of the circular plate would have been equidistant from the top and bottom of the drawer-front, and as the hole for the bolt was at the top of this plate it must always have been above the centre-line. If, therefore, this hole was enlarged to take the Victorian handle, this also would be nearer the top than the bottom. Second-ly, the base of the circular plate was pierced with a small hole through which a thin brass nail was driven into the wood to hold the plate against the surface when the ring-handle was lifted. Some trace of the resultant hole in the drawer-front should be discernible below the later wooden handle on close examination.

The deliberate re-veneering of the surface would, of course, conceal such external evidence though it would normally involve the obvious renewal of all the cock-beading, but would have no effect on the appearance of the inside, which should always be carefully scrutinised.

'Chippendale' chairs were also extensively made in the second half of the 19th century, and display sound craftsmanship and excellent materials, but there is usually a subtle strangeness about their proportions and details, apart from the surface-quality of the wood, which serves as a warning.

More dangerous than these are full sets of ostensible 18th-century or Regency chairs which have been formed by extending a small, genuine nucleus by cannibalisation. Usually, every chair in such a set will consist of old and new parts mixed together, and it will be necessary to examine not only the legs and backs but also the bottoms and insides of the seat-rails. If the last have been covered with hessian, as is often the case with overstuffed chairs, a written guarantee should always be requested. Naturally, attempting to pass off as original, chairs which have been treated in such a fashion within the knowledge of the vendor, constitutes fraud, and this will bring the dealer within the penal code; nevertheless, there is no doubt that it has been done.

In the late 19th and early 20th centuries, furniture showing strong neo-classical influence enjoyed a considerable vogue. It was not intended to deceive anyone and was often beautifully made, but now and again examples have a superficial similarity to comparable pieces of the late 18th century. Chief among these are Pembroke tables and small writing tables with superstructures at the rear of the tops.

The Pembroke tables are not only usually too small and totally lacking in patine, but the fly-brackets supporting the flaps, and the sides of the drawers are very often stained. This was never done in the Adam period. The same can be said of the drawers in the friezes of the writing tables, and the marquetry ornament sometimes found is mostly of a nondescript character. Some of them have panels of looking-glass let into the front of the superstructure, and there is no doubt about the late origin of these.

Experts themselves are sometimes at a loss to decide whether a piece of furniture is authentic or not, so no amateur need feel ashamed at being brought to a stand on occasions. Judgment becomes matured by experience, and the only satisfactory course is to study the subject and reinforce academic knowledge by looking at as much genuine antique furniture as possible.

A

Acanthus: in applied art signifies the formalised rendering of the leaf of the plant *acanthus spinosus* as it appears on the capitals of Corinthian columns; widely used on furniture from the renaissance to the 19th century.

and other ornaments of this kind were much used in the early 18th century and were occasionally of solid silver, though these have often become separated from the pieces of furniture they once embellished.

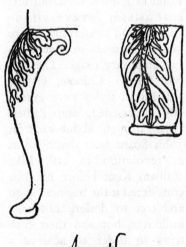

Acanthus

Acroteria (sing: acroterium): pedestals for statuettes above the cornices of cabinets, etc., often loosely extended to include the figures themselves; an architectural term. Figures

Acroteria

Act of Parliament Clock: a popular name for a type of wall clock with large, unglazed circular face, hanging in inns and other places of public resort and named from an Act of 1797 which imposed a tax on all kinds of timepieces and therefore discouraged their possession by private persons. As a result, large numbers of people disposed of their clocks and watches, and innkeepers soon discovered that business was greatly stimulated by the presence of a clock in an inn as it was often the only place where people could find out the time. During the currency of the Act great damage was suffered by the British horological industry, but although the statute was repealed within a year, the type had become popular and continued to be made, usually, however, with a glazed dial.

Adam, Robert (1728–1792): celebrated Scottish architect chiefly responsible for the introduction of the classical revival style into England after his return, in 1758, from a four-year visit to Italy. While there he became acquainted with the discoveries made during the excavations of Herculaneum (begun 1738) and Pompeii (begun 1755): classical cities near Naples which had been overwhelmed simultaneously by an eruption of Vesuvius in A.D. 79. Far from destroying these cities, the covering of volcanic ash or lava had actually preserved them, not only from the ravages of the elements, but also from the inroads of local populations, who commonly use abandoned, an-

cient towns as a source of building material, and either convert any artefacts to their own use or throw them away. Here, for the first time in history, were assembled household furniture, domestic utensils both useful and decorative and decorations chiefly in the form of wall-paintings, all of which provided cogent evidence of the material details of classical life.

Adam returned to practice in London fired with a burning enthusiasm for everything classical and a determination to adapt classical ornament to contemporary usage. The current rococo, Chinese, Gothic and mixed styles were gradually superseded, and Robert Adam brought about what Sir John Soane later described as a 'revolution in art'. Like William Kent before him, he considered it the business of an architect to design, not only buildings, but also their contents in order to achieve a harmonious consistency, and his designs for furniture, domestic silver, etc., exerted a vast influence, even bringing about the conversion, in some instances, of medieval castles and Tudor mansions into classical palaces.

In the 1760s Thomas Chippendale was commissioned by Adam to make furniture to his designs, and this was some of the best furniture that Chippendale ever made. Lightness and elegance took the place of the broad robustness of the rococo period and an admirable balance was achieved between strength and weight. Legs, for example, tapered downwards, so that the thickest part of the member was where it was needed—at the joint. If a piece of movable furniture is too heavy it tends to pull itself to pieces with its own weight, but furniture of the Adam period was graceful, light and strong. The style associated with Adam's name, involving classical decorative elements such as (*q.v.*) paterae, medallions, husks, swags, urns, beading, fluting, rams' heads, etc., prevailed until the end of the 18th century. In the 1780s, however, vernacular versions began to appear which, while retaining to an obvious degree the same innate feeling, were increasingly modified, diluted, and purged of their more noticeable classical content. Adam himself had designed chairs with oval backs which clearly derived their inspiration from medallions, and this type continued; but far more numerous were chair-backs shaped like shields which had no classical counterpart. These changes were reflected in the designs of Hepplewhite and Sheraton (*q.q.v.*), but however original these gifted men may have supposed they were, their work owed its basic character to the conceptions of Robert Adam.

At the end of the century a reaction set in. Men like Horace Walpole began to attack the Adam style in extravagant terms which represented little more than a rationalisation of their own boredom with something which, however excellent, had at last become wearisome to them. This reaction in taste in influential circles ushered in the so-called Regency style, but looking back over a longer perspective we can now see that the style which owed its introduction chiefly to the exertions of Robert Adam was one of the finest in the history of domestic furniture.

Alder: a timber much in demand for the manufacture of gunpowder but also used in the 18th century for provincial furniture. The wood has a persistent pinkish tinge and a strongly-marked figure in the grain.

Amboyna: a wood imported from the Caribbean area in the 18th century and used as veneer, either alone or contrasted with other woods in cross-banding. It has a richly-figured grain and is light brown in colour.

Anthemion: conventional ornamental motif of classical origin existing in several versions mostly deriving from the honeysuckle flower; chiefly prevalent during the late 18th and early 19th centuries. In the latter period this ornament was often applied in the form of ormolu of excellent quality.

Apple: timber from apple trees was often employed for carved work in the 17th century owing to its fine, homo-

Anthemion ornament

geneous grain. It was also used for veneers and inlay.

Apron: a decorative downward extension on the seat rail of a chair, the frieze of a table, stand, etc., and the underframe of a chest of drawers or cabinet. Aprons occurred on chairs in the last decade of the 17th century and continued on furniture of all kinds throughout the 18th century.

Apron (rococo)

Ash: a timber with something of the appearance of plain oak, used for drawer-linings from the 17th century and for country-made chairs in the 18th century. The diarist John Evelyn records that certain cuts of ash, taken no doubt from excrescences on the trunk, had an unusually interesting grain and were called 'green ebony' by 17th-century cabinet-makers who greatly esteemed it. It was also sometimes used in the form of veneer in the late 18th century.

Astragal: a narrow, semicircular moulding; the term is often erroneously applied to the glazing bars of bookcases, china cabinets, etc., though they are seldom of half-round section.

Aumbry (Ambry, Almery, Armoire): a word which, since the middle ages, has denoted various kinds of wooden storage structures provided with doors, including large presses for vestments, cabinets for books and small enclosed parts of early cupboards (*q.v.*). It fell out of general use in the early 17th century when the word 'cupboard' began to be widely used in its modern sense, but it is still a convenient term for the central compartment, closed by hinged doors, which occurs on some court cupboards (*q.v.*).

B

Baby Cage (Baby Walker, Go-Cart): possibly an Italian invention and certainly known in Germany in the 15th century, baby cages were not common in England until after 1600. They were used to teach infants to walk and consisted essentially of a top either ring-shaped or rectangular with a circular hole, capable of being opened and loosely closed round the child's body, connected by outward-splaying legs to a lower frame mounted

(Bachelor's chest

on wheels or castors. The earliest had four wheels which enabled the cage to move only backward and forward, but swivelling castors were introduced in the second half of the 17th century which permitted movement in any direction. The top ring was either covered with cloth or left plain. They remained widely popular until about 1800.

(Baby-cage

Bachelor's Chest: a convenient modern descriptive term, of doubtful authenticity, describing a small chest of drawers, current throughout the 18th century, with a fold-over top, hinged in front and supported on runners like those of a bureau (*q.v.*), providing a surface for writing, etc.

Back-Stool: in the 16th century the widespread triangular stool, which had been common since the 14th century, sometimes had one of the legs prolonged upwards to form a rest, and this was probably the origin of the term 'back-stool'. From about 1600 it was applied to a chair without arms, and

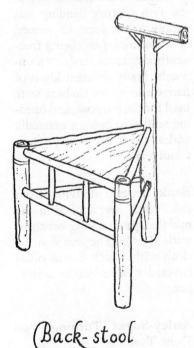

(Back-stool

continued to be used in this manner until about the middle of the 18th century when references occurred to 'back-stool chairs'. Since, however, the word 'armchair' had already been in use for some time before this, it soon became evident that it was unnecessary to differentiate further, and the modern usage became generally current.

Bailey and Saunders: a firm of cabinet-makers commissioned by the Prince of Wales (the future George IV) to provide certain items of magnificent furniture for Brighton Pavilion, including, in particular, four splendid carved and gilt chairs of Imperial Roman aspect. These and other items are preserved in the Royal collection.

Ball Foot: a spherical foot occurring on furniture chiefly in the second half of the 17th century, though it sometimes appeared on joined stools before 1600.

Ball-and-Claw Foot: see Claw-and-ball foot.

Baluster: one of the elements of a classical architectural balustrade which consisted of rows of balusters; typically of circular section, narrow above and bulbous below, much used as a detail of furniture from the renaissance onwards in either true or inverted form.

Baluster

Bamboo: occasionally used for furniture in the early 19th century, but commoner in the

simulated form for which turned beech was used from about 1770 to the late Regency. The British-made version was painted and was chiefly employed in a 'Chinese' décor, especially in bedrooms.

Banding: a decorative border, on or near the edge of a piece of furniture, often consisting, on oak pieces of the 16th and 17th centuries, of small inlaid squares of contrasting tone. After the general introduction of walnut in the second half of the 17th century banding was mainly in the form of veneer, cross-banding (*q.v.*) being frequently employed from then onwards. Many different kinds of native and exotic timbers were used for the purpose, and banding tended to become generally wider than previously from about 1750.

Bank: a term deriving from the French *banc* applied in the middle ages to a long bench or settle (*q.v.*). The cushion or cloth with which it was often covered was known as a banker.

Barley-Sugar Turning: see Twist-Turning.

Barometer (Baroscope, Weather-Glass): an apparatus embodying a column of mercury which records variations in atmospheric pressure from which imminent changes in the weather may be deduced, originating from a discovery by Evangelista Torricelli in 1643. After 1660, barometers were devised by English scientists, members of the Royal Society, whose exertions were encouraged by the scientific interests of Charles II. Famous contemporary clockmakers such as Daniel Quare and Thomas Tompion translated the inherent principles into practical form, so that what had been

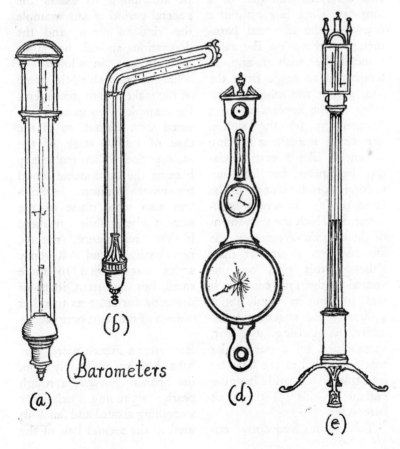

(a)

(b)

Barometers

(d)

(e)

scientific instruments took on the status of pieces of domestic furniture.

Their popularity continually increased. The chief domestic varieties were (*a*) the cistern barometer, housed in a narrow, vertical case attached to the wall and often provided with a hood, supported in front on two columns, like that of a long-case clock but without a dial; (*b*) the diagonal barometer, working on the same principle but with an arm extending at an angle from the top, giving the whole something of the appearance of a boomerang; (*c*) the siphon barometer, sometimes looking outwardly like a vertical cistern barometer, but later occurring more frequently in the form of (*d*) the wheel barometer, in which the movement of the column of mercury was amplified on a circular dial; although this type was invented in the 17th century, it was uncommon until about 1760; (*e*) the standing barometer, comprising a pillar, surmounted by a rectangular top, supported at the base by four splayed feet, and a hanging variant of this (*f*) the stick barometer.

The most frequently en-countered of the above types are naturally those of the mahogany period, the wheel barometer being especially prevalent from the late 18th to the early 19th century. The cistern type was popular on ships, where it was attached to the wall of a cabin by a gimbal to offset the motion of the vessel. In attempting to assess the general period of any example the kind of wood and the decoration should be taken into account, in addition to other factors such as the name of the maker. Early specimens, for example, were usually veneered with walnut, as in the case of cabinet-work of the same period. When mahogany became the fashionable wood for other furniture, barometers also were made of the same timber, while ornament in the renaissance, rococo, neo-classical and Regency styles was applied to these small, but important, items of domestic furniture as to other objects of the same periods.

Baroque: a French word, perhaps deriving ultimately from the Spanish *barrueco*, a rough pearl, signifying originally something absurd and fanciful; used in the second half of the

19th century to denote certain elaborate ornament and styles characteristic of the late renaissance, for example, carving of the reign of Charles II and architectural forms and decoration applied to furniture in the second quarter of the 18th century. It was virtually the final manifestation of the renaissance style, but in its last phase it included a great deal of dynamic scroll-work and this merged into the rococo, so that it is sometimes difficult to define the exact line of demarcation in the transitional phase.

Bases: indicating, apart from its general significance, the valances round the lower parts of beds from the second half of the 17th century onwards, and probably deriving, by analogy, from the gathered skirts, sometimes simulated in armour, worn by men in the early 16th century and denoted by the same term.

Bason Stand: an 18th-century term for various forms of what would now be called a washstand, the modern spelling 'basin' being generally employed from about 1780. The

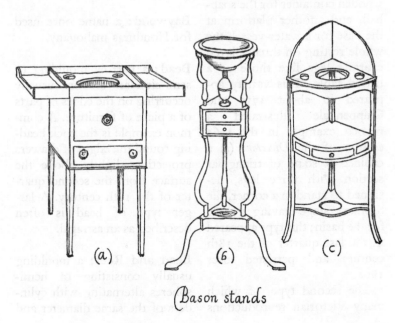

(a)   *(b)*   *(c)*

Bason stands

three main types, which admitted of great variety within their category, were as follows: (*a*) an enclosed structure on four legs, with the hole in the top for the basin covered by two lateral, hinged flaps, meeting in the centre; occurring no earlier than about 1735 and continuing throughout the 18th century; (*b*) an open stand consisting of three vertical supports, usually curvaceous, with a wooden ring at the top for the basin, a platform beneath this containing one or two triangular drawers and often surmounted by an ovoid wooden container for the soap-ball, and another platform at the base for a water-vessel, the whole resting on three splayed cabriole legs like those of a tripod table. This variety appeared in about 1750 and Chippendale illustrated a rococo example in the 1762 edition of the *Director*; (*c*) a cabinet or stand of triangular section with three legs, designed to stand in a corner, the topmost stage having a hole for the basin; this type appeared in the last quarter of the 18th century and persisted after 1800.

The second type, of which many Victorian reproductions were made, is often erroneously described as a wig-stand (*q.v.*).

Bas-Relief (Italian, *basso-rilievo***)**: carving on architecture or furniture in which the ornament projects less than half its normal height above the surface. Beyond this it is called high-relief (*alto-rilievo*).

Battlemented: a term generally applicable to medieval case-furniture only, denoting a cornice embellished with merlons and crenelles deriving from contemporary military architecture.

Baywood: a name once used for Honduras mahogany.

Bead: a narrow moulding of semi-circular section usually occurring on the edges of parts of a piece of furniture. A common example is the cock beading round the edges of drawers projecting slightly above the surface from the second quarter of the 18th century. A larger type of bead is often described as an astragal.

Bead and Reel: a moulding usually consisting of hemispheres alternating with cylinders of the same diameter and

Bead and Reel

about three times the length. It occurred in the form of inlay in the first half of the 16th century, and was common on mahogany furniture from before the middle of the 18th century. The lower parts of the cornices of mirrors of the late 18th and early 19th centuries often displayed this decoration, usually with the cylinders spirally grooved.

Beading (Bead Moulding): ornament of classical origin, consisting of rows of small, contiguous hemispheres, found on architecture, silver, furniture, etc., in the late 18th century. It sometimes occurred on chair backs, the arm-stumps (supports), and down the centres of legs.

Bearer: a central supporting member, running from back to front of the base of a long drawer, with a groove on each side into which the two halves of the bottom panel are slotted; used from the late 18th century.

Beds: so much importance was attached to beds in the middle ages that they sometimes formed the subject of specific bequests in contemporary wills, but it is often clear from the context that the term was applied to the bedding and hangings, if any, rather than the wooden structures that

C.1580

supported them. Even in only moderately wealthy households beds were commonly sited beneath canopies or testers of fabric which were suspended from the ceiling by cords. As rooms containing beds were used as what we should now call reception rooms when they were not being slept-in, the

13

curtains were usually looped up at the foot into a pear-shaped bag so that the bed could be reclined on or used as a seat.

It is evident from contemporary paintings that bedposts were commonplace in Italy in the second half of the 15th century, but although they

c.1740

were known in England at the same time they were extremely rare until after 1500. At first they always consisted of upward extensions of the legs of the bedstock (bedstead) with a low panel at the rear, but as the century advanced the front posts were often made free-standing, and both types continued into the 17th century.

By 1530 the rear panel had increased to the height of the tester, which was now generally of wooden panelling instead of cloth, and as the rear posts were no longer essential, their function was gradually taken over by the vertical stiles which enclosed the panels of the bedhead. Surviving specimens from the early 16th century enable us to see that the bedstocks were pierced round the sides with holes through which cords were passed to support the mattress, which might be filled with feathers, wool, straw or leaves.

Early posts were of no great girth and might be carved with simple ornament such as chevrons, or renaissance motifs, but in the second half of the 16th century the familiar Elizabethan vase-shaped protuberance appeared, often capped with radial gadroons (q.v.), and this continued for some years after 1600. In the early 17th century the florid ebulliance of the Elizabethan forms progressively waned with the passage of time, their place being taken by simple baluster turnings of less pronounced character. The posts were reunited with the bedstocks and, after the Restoration, increased greatly in height, the attendant hangings displaying a magnificence of slightly funereal solemnity sometimes enhanced by plumed cornices covered with fabric, and tassels. Cornices gradually assumed a less cluttered appearance in the early 18th century, and shortly before 1700 appeared the 'Angel' bed which lacked the front posts, the tester, lighter than its appearance suggested, being supported by thin chains from the ceiling or brackets at the rear.

During the Palladian revival, associated with the name of William Kent (*q.v.*), treatment was often strongly architectural, the mahogany cornices generally being wholly or partly unconcealed by cloth, with simple dentil mouldings or gadrooned edges. In the next stylistic phase, rococo ornament was chiefly confined to cornices in the Chippendale period, often with very pleasing effect, and at the same time many beds were made in the Chinese fashion, with testers covered by pagoda-like roofs and headboards fretted in the same manner as chairbacks, but on a larger scale. In the Adam period the cornices were once more generally concealed, and

nearly always had shaped, pendant valances which emerged from beneath. These parts were commonly embellished with neo-classical motifs such as paterae and swags (*q.q.v.*), while the centre of the canopy often rose in the form of a dome,

c. 1785

supported on a light internal framework. Both Hepplewhite and Sheraton (*q.q.v.*) illustrated designs for beds and also 'bed pillars', the latter being mostly of mahogany but sometimes of satinwood. The beds were in the same general style as those designed by Robert Adam, sometimes with centrally-domed canopies, and the valances beneath the cornices and at the bases were often looped up at intervals in a manner suggestive of swags, or had applied ribbon, etc., which produced a similar effect.

Hepplewhite's designs showed his usual restraint, but Sheraton's were more adventurous though sometimes less practical. One design, for an 'Alcove Bed', shows the outside curving inward at the centre in a manner which evinces scant regard for human anatomy, while in another entitled 'An Eliptic Bed for a Single Lady', the balance is redressed to such a degree that ample accommodation is afforded for an occupant with pelvic development of a very remarkable sort, though it is only fair to say that the fault lies less with the design than with the title. Yet another design illustrates 'A Summer Bed in Two Compartments', in which two separate couches, enclosed within the same structure, are approached by a central gangway which is entered through a round-headed triumphal arch. Though some of these conceptions may seem somewhat comical at the present day, they

nevertheless bear witness to the questing vigour of late 18th-century design, and nearly all, in varying degree, acknowledged their indebtedness to the prevailing architectural mode despite the dilution of the original pure, neo-classical spirit by exponents of its vernacular versions. Hepplewhite's bed posts were elegant in shape, but carved ornament was often confined to a protuberance just above the level of the bedclothes, where it frequently consisted of nothing more than a zone of the familiar stiff, formal leafage so often found on contemporary silver hollowware. Sheraton's were more elaborate, and were mostly carved all over. Their ornament included, not only the usual neo-classical details such as fluting, husks, etc., but also reeding (q.v.), both straight and spiralled.

All-over spiral reeding, increasingly coarser in section than that of the late 18th century, occurred on bed-posts of the early 19th century as on other furniture. It must be regarded as an unfortunate innovation, arising only from a restless desire for continual change, as it tended to vitiate the elegant perpendicularity of the member to which it was applied. Beds of the Regency period seemed to exemplify the evolution of design in two contradictory aspects. Either they were chaste and severe in accordance with the prevailing doctrinaire approach to late classicism, or they were clumsily frivolous in a manner which implied a lack of aesthetic restraint and presaged the coming Victorian decadence.

Bedstaff: (*a*) a short rod, several of which were stuck in holes along the top of the sides of a bedstock to keep the bedding from slipping off, and (*b*) a staff for levelling a feather, etc., bed when making it.

Bedstock: the framework of a bed; a bedstead.

Beech: a native English wood much used for cheaper furniture from about 1660 onwards, being often ebonised or coloured to simulate the fashionable but more expensive walnut in the late 17th century. It was always in great demand as a base for painted ornament. Its homogeneous texture makes it convenient to work, but it is very subject to attack by wood-worm. Because of this, John Evelyn expressed the view, in the reign of Charles II, that its use should be forbidden by law, but it continued to recommend itself, not only because it was in plentiful supply, but also because it seemed extravagant to many people to cover more costly timbers with paint.

Bell Flower Ornament: rows of usually three-petalled flower heads sometimes carved in low relief on furniture in the late 18th century, and often practically indistinguishable from contemporary neoclassical husks. Another variant consisted of a broader, more

open blossom, sometimes used singly to fill in spaces.

Benches (Forms): movable benches were common in the middle ages together with a fixed variety which was attached to the wall and considered as an integral part of the building, but no examples have survived from before the 15th century. Gothic specimens show certain affinities with contemporary architecture, having rails cut into pointed arches and slab-like end-standards shaped at the edges to look like buttresses. Modified versions of these, conformable to Tudor architecture, continued into the 16th century, but the advent of renaissance influence brought about a more curvaceous treatment of under-frames. Wooden benches are found mentioned in Elizabethan documents, but examples originating in the hundred years from the second half of the 16th century are scarce, less because of the accidents to which antique objects are prone than because contemporary joined stools (*q.v.*) were more numerous owing to their greater convenience and the fact that they could be stowed away under the table after meals. Enough

have remained, however, for it to be seen that benches followed the same stylistic evolution as their smaller relatives, and may therefore be considered as elongated versions of stools, recognisable by the presence of the same details.

Bergère: a French term, anglicised in various ways in the first half of the 18th century when the object it described was introduced into England. It seems that some uncertainty may have prevailed in the application of the word, which appears to have indicated both an armchair and a settee. In present-day terminology it denotes either, when the back, seat and space below the arms are filled with woven split cane, and some support is given this usage by a reference in 1771 to a 'burgier' with 'cane back and seat'. Loose, fitted cushions were provided, one lying on the seat and another leaning against the back. Bergères continued into the 19th century when they enjoyed a good deal of popularity, their legs, with noticeable frequency, being decorated with reeding.

Bible Box: a term popularly applied to any large oak box, with hinged lid, of 17th-century date, though the ancestry of the type is traceable to the middle ages. Although some were undoubtedly made primarily to contain bibles, most

Bible box

were used for general storage, so that it is usually impossible to be dogmatic about the purpose of any particular example. Some had sloping lids which suggests that they were used for writing, and these are often called 'Derbyshire desks', though there is no reason to suppose that their manufacture was confined to that county. Others, of similar construction, were heavily carved, and this would have made it practically impossible to use them as desks. All were easily portable and could be stood on any convenient flat surface, but some were supported on specially-made four-legged stands, some of which have survived.

Birch: a native English timber which had a bad reputation as a furniture-wood in the 17th century, but was nevertheless used by provincial makers for chairs, etc., after 1700. In the late 18th century, when satinwood (*q.v.*) was fashionable for furniture of the best quality, birch, both British and American, was occasionally used as a cheaper substitute, mostly in the form of veneer but sometimes in the solid.

Boarded Chest: a popular name for a chest made from six planks of oak or other wood: one for the top, two for the sides, one for the base and two for the ends. The last were extended downwards to form supports, usually with a piece of roughly inverted V-shape cut out of the base of each.

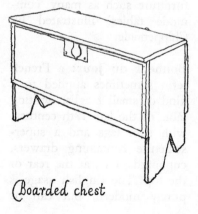

Boarded chest

19

Though of deceptively ancient appearance, most were poor relations of the panelled chest and occurred chiefly in the 17th and 18th centuries especially in the provinces.

Bobbin Turning: decorative turning of bobbin-form occurring chiefly in the mid-17th century on the legs of chairs and tables.

Bolection Moulding: a curved, projecting moulding of ogee section surrounding a panel; occasionally found on furniture from the early 17th century, but later occurring more usually on doors or wall-panelling.

Bombé: a French term denoting, in England, the outward-swelling form of a piece of furniture such as many 'commode tables' illustrated by Chippendale.

Bonheur du Jour: a French term sometimes applied to a kind of small English writing table of the late 18th century, with slim legs and a super-structure containing drawers, cupboards, etc., at the rear of the top. The English usage is purely modern, but can be

justified on the ground that it serves to distinguish the type thus designated from others, the term 'writing table' being of excessively catholic application and including, for example, ponderous flat library tables of a totally different character.

Bookcases: domestic bookcases, apart from hanging shelves, did not, so far as is known, exist before 1660 in England, and those made for Samuel Pepys in 1666, now in Magdalene College, Cambridge, are probably the earliest to survive. A few are known

Bookcase c.1730

mounted on legs with the exaggerated turnings characteristic of the last decade of the 17th century, but they were never anything but rare until after 1700. Walnut was occasionally employed in the early 18th century, but so great an expanse of timber was required that cheaper woods, sometimes painted, were used throughout the 18th century as well as mahogany. The latter gained in popularity for such large objects from about 1740, and examples from this period were conceived in the heavy architectural manner associated with the Earl of Burlington and William Kent, and often had fronts like the entrance to a Palladian building with a central arch and a subsidiary one on each side, and a massive broken pediment (*q.v.*) above the centre of the cornice.

Thereafter, large bookcases were generally of breakfront type, with the major central portion projecting beyond a smaller wing on each side, though straight fronts were never wholly neglected. They were supported chiefly on low, solid plinths, but bracket feet, varying in number with the size of the case, had been used since the early 18th century and

never went entirely out of fashion. From about 1750, relief ornament of rococo type was sometimes found on larger wooden surfaces such as the doors which often enclosed the lower parts, and this was succeeded, in the classical-revival era, by ornament of neo-classical character. An existing example designed by Robert Adam has large horizontal oval paterae (*q.v.*) on the lower central doors, the shape being chosen to fit oblong spaces; similar doors on the wings, being square, bear paterae of circular shape. The central frieze has swags of husks (*q.v.*) and small paterae, the wings having short, vertical flutes. Dentil (*q.v.*) mouldings run beneath the cornices and the whole is surmounted by a broken triangular pediment.

In the late 18th century it became a frequent practice to fill the upper doors of large bookcases with brass trellis, and this persisted into the early 19th century on an increasing scale. Typical Regency details appeared on bookcases as on other furniture. Pilasters (*q.v.*), for example, might have an Egyptian head at the top and feet emerging at the base, or

21

they might consist of hocked animal legs crowned by an appropriate head, usually a lion's. Rosewood was widely used as an alternative to mahogany and brass inlay often occurred as decoration. Monumental breakfront bookcases continued to be made, but a more modestly-conceived domestic type appeared in a low, horizontal form, sometimes no more than 3 ft. high. These were often of open construction, without doors or glazing. George Smith (*q.v.*), in his volume *A Collection of Designs for Household Furniture and Decoration,* published in 1808, shows long, low bookcases with a pedestal for a bust at each end, and recommends that glazed doors should be backed with silk in certain circumstances. In practice, this silk was often pleated and fronted with brass trellis instead of glass.

In the very late 18th century a taller variety of open bookcase was already in use, and was designed to fill the space between two windows not otherwise occupied by a pier glass and pier table (*q.v.*), but these became considerably more numerous in the 19th century. The small revolving bookcase

mounted on a central pillar, so popular in the early 20th century, made its first appearance in about 1800, and a design was patented by Crosby in 1808. As the tiers of shelves were of circular shape, thin, triangular-section blocks were inserted at intervals, often backed with imitation book-spines.

Bow Front: the curving, convex front of a chest of drawers, etc., first fashionable in the late 18th century and extensively reproduced in the Victorian era.

Boxwood: a pale, hard wood, with a specific gravity higher

Bow-fronted Chest of Drawers

than that of water, which polishes to a light brown colour; much used for inlay on 16th-century oak furniture and for marquetry in the late 17th century; again employed in the late 18th century for inlay, especially in the form of stringing.

Boys and Crowns: contemporary name for a type of ornament occurring particularly on the cresting rails of chairs and consisting of a crown flanked by naked children; used extensively from 1660 and throughout the reign of Charles II, it bore witness to the almost universal relief at the restoration of the monarchy after years of puritanism.

Bracket Foot: a foot to a piece of case furniture straight or ogee-shaped on the outside but spanning the inner angle in the form of a bracket, and consisting of two pieces of wood joined vertically at the corner. It is evident from contemporary engravings that bracket feet were known in Germany in the early 16th century, but although renaissance influence reached England chiefly from this source, feet of this kind were virtually un-known until the late 17th century.

Braganza Foot: see Spanish Foot.

Bramah Lock: a lock in which the key acts upon a rotating cylinder, invented by Joseph Bramah in 1784 but more frequent in the 19th century.

Brass Inlay: the decoration of English furniture by metal inlay was practised sparsely in the late 17th century and probably by a single practitioner, Gerreit Jensen, who worked for the Crown and certain of the aristocracy. In the first half of the 18th century its incidence may have been higher than surviving examples appear to suggest, for a pair of large bookcases at Powderham Castle, Devon, made by a local craftsman in 1740, are inlaid with brass. For most of the 18th century, however, the technique seems to have been left in abeyance, and there is no doubt that its boldness of effect would have been incongruous with the neo-classical style; but Sheraton, in his *Cabinet Dictionary* of 1803, refers approvingly to 'the present mode of inlaying with brass', so it must have been quite re-established by then. In the first quarter of the 19th century it was very frequently employed in the form either of stringing, or fret-cut designs of varying elaboration, and was found on all kinds of furniture including chairs. Rosewood and mahogany were the chief woods to which it was applied, but it also occurred on chairs made of beech, stained to simulate rosewood.

Breakfast Table: a small, four-legged mahogany table with two hinged flaps supported, in the raised position, on fly brackets, and stretchers or a lower stage often partly enclosed by 'Chinese' fret. Chip-

Breakfast Table
(Chippendale Design)

pendale illustrated an example in the third edition of the *Director* (1762), but they are somewhat rare owing to the short period of their popularity.

Breakfront: a term applied to a piece of case furniture, usually large, divided vertically into a number of sections one or more of which project in front of those on either side, thus breaking the line. Familiar examples are the Georgian library bookcases with, typically, a wide central portion standing out in advance of the narrower side-wings.

Broken Pediment: see Pediment.

Brushing Slide: a modern term, probably erroneous, used to describe the pull-out slides sometimes occurring just below the tops of chests of drawers and commodes from early in the 18th century; mostly either in plain, polished wood or covered with green baize, and probably used for writing. Some late 18th-century designs for dressing chests show a drawer on one side with a basin for washing, and a drawer on the other side containing writing facilities, so the latter must have been considered desirable in a bedroom.

Buffet: a word of French origin occurring occasionally in England in 16th-century records, such references being too imprecise for an exact meaning to be deduced. At the same time an English word, spelt in the same manner, was used as a variant of the old adjective 'buffed', that is, stuffed or padded, but the noun, indicating a piece of furniture, is now employed in two main senses. (*a*) As a synonym for 'court cupboard' (*q.v.*). Even if there was ever any warrant for this usage it must be considered undesirable, as there is no doubt that 'cupboard'—in its original sense—was the term in general use at the time when such pieces were fashionable. (*b*) From the beginning of the 18th century it denoted the coved wall-recesses fitted with shelves for the display of porcelain, which were found in most houses of any size. These recesses were built into the panelling but Sheraton, in his *Cabinet Dictionary* of 1803, used the word to describe a free-standing cabinet enclosed by two doors and

Bureau

surmounted by tiers of shelves. This represents a reasonable extension of the earlier sense.

Bun Foot: a foot in the form of a flattened sphere of any size, on the leg of a cabinet, chest of drawers, table, etc., in the second half of the 17th century.

Bureau: this term has been used in so many different ways that no definition can be entirely historically satisfying, and the best solution is to follow Sheraton, who strengthens the most widespread modern usage by stating, in his *Cabinet Dictionary* (1803), that the word has 'generally been applied to common desks with drawers under them'. He adds that when such a desk is surmounted by a bookcase it is called a bureau bookcase.

Since notions may vary as to what constitutes a 'common' desk, it should be mentioned that the type in question is closed by a sloping fall, hinged at its base, which swings outward to a horizontal position where it is supported on runners (lopers). The design first appeared in about 1690, mounted on legs rather than drawers, and these early specimens should perhaps be called 'desks on stands'; before the end of the 17th century, however, the normal bureau was gaining in popular esteem which increased after 1700. As in the case of other furniture of the period, the best examples were veneered with walnut and might be mounted on ball, bun, or bracket feet. The first two had fallen out of general use by about 1715, and bracket feet remained standard for the remainder of the 18th century, though examples supported on cabriole legs of varying height from the early part of the century terminated in feet of all the different kinds found on other types of furniture, including chairs, with legs of the same type. In addition to decorative

techniques involving the use only of wood, such as oystering, marquetry (*q.q.v.*), etc., painted decoration in the form of 'japanning' was applied to some bureaux, with or without bookcases or cabinets on top, the designs being of Chinese inspiration. The background colours were chiefly red, green or black, with the motifs in gold or silver, and the effect is often extremely sumptuous. This fashion did not outlast the first quarter of the 18th century.

Up to about 1740, the small drawers and compartments contained in these desks curved forward at both ends with noticeable frequency, leaving a space between them in the form of a bay. Thereafter, they tended to be in a straight line parallel with the front plane. The bookcases or cabinets which often accompanied bureaux had door panels of wood or looking-glass until after the middle of the 18th century. These were increasingly superseded by clear glass mounted in glazing bars arranged in patterns which were miniature versions of those found on contemporary library bookcases, and most of the bookcases on bureaux of the mahogany period are of this type.

As examples of the uncertainty prevailing in the terminology of the subject may be mentioned the fact that Chippendale called a bureau bookcase a 'desk and bookcase', and a dressing-table with a writing surface inside the top drawer a 'buroe dressing-table'. The definition used in this section is therefore narrower than that justified by Georgian usage, but unless reasonable limits are imposed terms are liable to become confused and almost meaningless.

Bureau Bookcase: a piece of case furniture, first introduced in the late 17th century, consisting of a bureau supporting a bookcase of the same width enclosed by doors which were first of wood or with mirror panels, later of clear glass.

Bureau Cabinet: similar in appearance to a bureau bookcase, but having a doored cabinet above the bureau for the storage of items other than books including shells, medals, etc. When the doors are closed the two are indistinguishable.

Bureau-Plat: a French term sometimes applied in England to a flat writing table, usually with the object of enhancing its importance. Writing tables of this kind appeared in France in the late 17th century and were popular in England in the second half of the 18th century. The use of the term is to be deplored.

Burr: an excrescence on the trunks of various trees filled with crowded, embryonic twigs incapable of increasing in length, which, when cut across, provides an intricately-figured veneer full of minute circles which are sections through the twigs. In cabinet-making burrs were chiefly confined to elm, yew, walnut, alder, oak and maple, and were used with

Butler's Tray

decorative effect from the 16th century onwards.

Butler's Tray (Standing Tray): a tray usually surrounded with a gallery containing hand-holes, mounted on legs or a folding X-stand, and popular from about 1720 until well into the 19th century; mostly of mahogany but sometimes of papier-mâché from the late 18th century, when the tray was occasionally oval or kidney-shaped instead of rectangular. A late 18th-century type, with a top which folded with the stand, is often incorrectly called a 'coaching table'.

Butterfly Hinge: a type of surface-hinge in use from the medieval period onwards having plates each side of the central barrel splaying out in a manner suggestive of butterflies' wings.

C

Cabinet-Makers: a term which came into use in England only in the second half of the 17th century, the ancestral sequence being carpenters, joiners, cabinet-makers, the last coinciding approximately with the advent of the age of elegance, in which technical and aesthetic accomplishment attained unprecedented heights.

Cabochon: oval-shaped ornament carved in relief in the 16th and 17th centuries, and again from about 1740 on the knees of cabriole legs and elsewhere on pieces of furniture, when there was sometimes an indentation on one side giving the motif a kidney-like appearance. The term derives from that describing a polished but unfaceted gem stone; for example, the Black Prince's ruby, still part of the British Crown jewels, and given to Edward, Prince of Wales, by Pedro of Castille in the 14th century, is a cabochon jewel.

Cabriole Leg: a furniture leg

with the external profile in the form of an ogee or flattened 'S', the outward curve at the top being known as the knee. When a chair-leg of this type has a tongue-shaped process extending upward from the knee it is known as 'hipped'. Legs of this kind, with or without the hip, were almost unchallenged in Britain in the first half of the 18th century, but continued in popularity for long after, especially in the French form with a scrolled foot. The shape was known in France in the 17th century, and

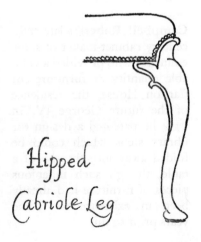

Hipped
Cabriole Leg

was probably introduced to English chair-makers by Daniel Marot, a distinguished French Huguenot designer, who eventually came to England after leaving France shortly before the persecutions of his co-religionists following the revocation of the Edict of Nantes by Louis XIV in 1685.

Caddy-Stand: a more correct name for what is wrongly called a Tea Poy (*q.v.*).

Calamander Wood: a mottled brown wood with black stripes, botanically related to ebony, imported from the East Indies from the late 18th century and used for veneer, chiefly in the form of banding, during the Regency.

Campbell, Robert: a late 18th-century cabinet-maker of some eminence who provided a valuable quantity of furniture for Carlton House, the residence of the future George IV. In 1774 he patented a design for library steps which could be folded away into the top of a table, though such ingenious pieces of furniture had already been in existence for some years prior to this.

Candle-Box: during the 17th century, candle-boxes were an integral part of most contemporary chests, and are now often erroneously considered as receptacles for pistols; but separate containers, usually of oak, were made as well, and these continued in use far into the 19th century, often with a pierced extension at the top to enable them to be hung on a nail.

Candle-Stand: the correct English term for what is sometimes described alternatively by the French word *torchère*: a wooden stand for a candlestick, candelabrum or lamp. Of pillar-and-claw form from about 1660, candle-stands were often shaped like classical tripods or pedestals in the late 18th century.

Caning: Malayan rattan cane was brought to England by the East India Company soon after the Restoration, and in split and woven form began to be used for seating furniture from early in the 1660s. The mesh was coarse at first, but had become fine by 1680. Its incidence began to decline in the 18th century until by 1740 it had almost fallen out of use,

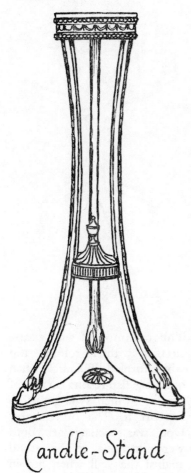

Candle-Stand

but it was restored to favour in the middle of the century with the introduction of chairs of Chinese character. Chippendale commented in this connection: 'They have commonly Cane-Bottoms, with loose Cushions'. Thereafter, woven split cane never ceased to be used for the seats of chairs.

Canted Corner: a bevelled corner on a piece of case furniture as an alternative to a right-angle; chiefly popular in the first half of the 18th century, the bevel could be plain, inlaid, fluted or reeded. Canted corners often occurred on the upper stages of tallboys in the early 18th century.

Canterbury: (*a*) an open-topped, partitioned music stand sometimes with a shallow drawer beneath, usually supported on four short legs; first introduced in the late 18th century; (*b*) a plate and cutlery stand with a semicircular end for the plates and divisions for cutlery and silver which appeared in the second half of the 18th century. Sheraton attempted to explain the term but its origin is, in fact, unknown.

Caquetoire Chair: a light chair with tall back, often carved, and a seat of D-shape, straight along the front, with arm-rests following the curve of the sides. The type was introduced from France in the first half of the 16th century and is somewhat uncommon. It was

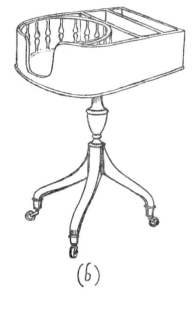

Canterburys (a)   (b)

devised especially for the use of ladies, the light construction enabling it to be moved easily. The name derives from the French verb *caqueter*, to gossip, and seems to have been given to these chairs by Parisian ladies.

Card-Tables: card games were originally played on any convenient flat surface, but in the last decade of the 17th century appeared small tables specifically designed for card-playing. They were initially of two main kinds and were made of walnut in common with all the best furniture of the same period.

The commoner was semi-circular with a folding top which formed a full circle when open, the flap resting on two of the legs which swung out to support it. The other, rarer type was rectangular. Both were intended to be stood against the wall when not in use, and this applied to nearly all card-tables throughout the Georgian period. A modified rectangular form was introduced in about 1710. Apart from the usual folding top it had four legs, one only of which hinged out at right-angles to the frame to serve as whether in walnut or mahogany. They persisted into the second half of the 18th century, the legs and other details evolving in accordance with coeval fashions affecting legged furniture in general. In the Chippendale period, for example, when chairs, tables, etc., often had straight, square legs with the inner angles chamfered off as an alternative to the cabriole, a severely rectangular card-table became fashionable in addition to other kinds. The frieze and legs were often blind-fretted with the sort of decoration common on contemporary 'Chinese' furniture, though not necessarily of authentic Chinese character. By

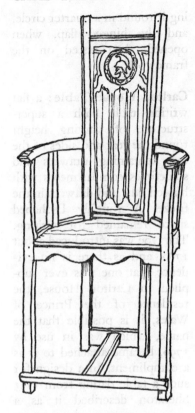

Caquetoire Chair

a support, though rare examples had a concertina action which enabled all the legs to be fixed. At each corner was a circular projection slightly dished to hold a candlestick, and on each of the four sides a hollow was provided for coins or tokens. Some of the finest of all card-tables are of this type,

Card-Table c. 1715

Card-Table c. 1810

1770 the platforms for candle-sticks and recesses for counters had passed out of general use. Both Hepplewhite and Sheraton illustrated designs showing tops shaped and decorated in the same idiom as various contemporary pier tables (*q.v.*), though it is probable that the vast majority actually manufactured were in plain mahogany. In the early 19th century, when pillar-and-claw supports were widely current, they often appeared on card-tables; but one of the most popular variants had four spider legs emerging from the corners of a small platform and above this rose four turned pillars surmounted by the folding top. This was prepared for playing by twist-

ing it round in a quarter circle, and the hinged flap, when opened, then rested on the framework.

Carlton House Table: a flat writing table with a super-structure of varying height round the rear and sides of the top containing drawers and sometimes compartments with hinged lids, and drawers in the frieze. A roughly D-shaped space remained for writing. The type was introduced about 1780, and as there is no evidence that one was ever supplied to Carlton House, the residence of the Prince of Wales, it is possible that the name, which was in use by 1796, became attached to it as a compliment. In a design for such a table dating from 1793 Sheraton described it as a

Carlton House Table

'Lady's Drawing and Writing Table'. Carlton House tables were popular in the late 18th and early 19th centuries, and were made in mahogany, satinwood and rosewood. Some excellent reproductions were made in the Victorian period.

Carolean: an adjective deriving from the Latin *Carolus*— Charles, which is not recommended as it can be applied with equal accuracy to the totally different styles of the reigns of Charles I (1625–1649) and Charles II (1660–1685).

Castors: small wheels or rollers attached to furniture to enable it more easily to be moved were unknown in England before the 17th century, but were evidently being made by a distinct class of tradesmen called 'castor-makers' by 1690. Early examples consisted of wooden wheels, and smaller boxwood balls and rollers were in use in the early 18th century. Before the middle of the century they were being made of compressed leather, and this material continued to be employed until after 1760 although brass castors had come into use before 1730. Records surviving from this period show that castors were sometimes fitted later to furniture originally supplied without them. Chippendale did not illustrate castors at all, but as much of the furniture of his time was undoubtedly equipped with them, the explanation is probably that it was presumed that a purchaser would please himself whether he specified them or not. Brass castors of many kinds were commonplace from about 1770.

Cat: a wooden or metal stand for keeping a dish warm in the fireplace, occurring from the mid-18th century. The best examples were of mahogany with three splayed cabriole legs like those of a contemporary

Cat

tripod-table, and three turned arms above forming the rest. The majority, however, had six identical turned arms, and from this type the name may have derived, owing to the fact that the stand would land on its feet whichever way it was set down.

Cavetto Moulding: a concave moulding found on the cornices of case furniture from the end of the 17th century, but commoner after 1700 when it tended to replace the more complicated torus (*q.v.*).

Cedar: though known in the 17th century, and recommended by John Evelyn, North American and West Indian cedar was not used on any considerable scale until after the middle of the 18th century, when it began to be employed to some extent for drawer-linings, but more frequently in clothes presses (*q.v.*) of good quality for the sliding shelves. It was probably considered that it discouraged clothes-moths, and the scent of the wood is often still much in evidence after the lapse of over two hundred years.

Cellaret: a receptacle to con-

tain bottles of wine; the term appears to have come into use in about 1740, replacing the name 'cellar' which had denoted similar objects from the late 17th century when they were first introduced. Mahogany cellarets, carved with decorative details typical of their periods, were sited beneath sideboard tables, and continued to be made in the 19th century, when they were often of sarcophagus form. The

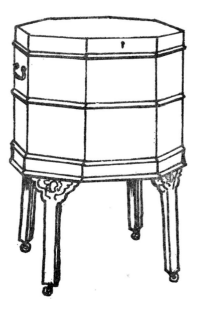

Cellaret

interior was generally divided into lead-lined compartments for bottles. In the late 18th century, when self-contained sideboards were introduced as an alternative to the variety without drawers but with an urn-crowned pedestal at each end, cellarets were embodied in sideboards, usually in a deep drawer. In the early 19th century they were sometimes called 'wine-keepers'.

Chairs: until well into the 18th century the term 'chair' was restricted to single seats with arms. Armchairs of a monumental, throne-like aspect occurred in the medieval period, but their possession was generally confined to nobles, prelates and wealthy merchants. In the 16th century they began to penetrate further down through the social scale, though in the Royal household, and noble households which copied the habits and conventions of the court, a rigid etiquette governed their use at least until the late 17th century.

Examples from the Elizabethan period (1558–1603) are occasionally encountered but survivals dating prior to the reign of James I (1603–1625) are rare. Armchairs of the late

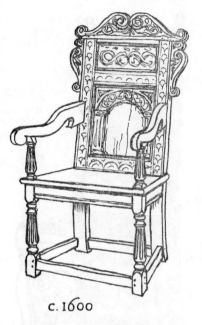

c. 1600

16th and early 17th centuries usually had panelled backs, often with a shaped cresting overriding the uprights with console-shaped projections below on each side. The front legs, prolonged upwards to support the arms, were turned in the form of attenuated balusters which were fluted or sometimes gadrooned; this ornament disappeared early in the 17th century, except in the provinces, the turnings thereafter being plain. Panelled armchairs of this kind continued into the second half of the 17th century, but were generally

bers until, from the beginning of the reign of Charles II (1660–1685), they became commonplace and were often used for dining instead of benches and joined stools (*q.v.*). Woven, split cane was employed for

c. 1670

superseded by the new French styles with twist-turning (*q.v.*) after the fashionable adoption of walnut in about 1660. Meanwhile, an armless chair or backstool (*q.v.*) had appeared in about 1600 in the shape of the farthingale chair (*q.v.*), after which chairs without arms were made in increasing num-

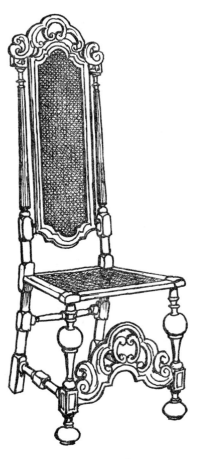

c. 1690

seats and usually backs as well, and this persisted until the end of the 17th century.

By the reign of James II (1685–1689) twist-turning had been replaced by straight turning embellished with slim balusters, but after the accession of William and Mary these were superseded by turnings of a more pronounced character, including the Portuguese Swell, the Mushroom, and the inverted Cup (*q.q.v.*), which were found on all kinds of legged furniture until after 1700. At the same period, chair-backs reached their maximum height in relation to their width.

The cabriole leg (*q.v.*) was introduced at the end of the 17th century but did not come into general use until the reign of Queen Anne (1702–1714), when the claw-and-ball foot (*q.v.*) also made its first appearance, becoming commoner in the reign of George I (1714–1727). From the time of the Restoration, the backs of chairs, between the uprights, had never made contact with the seat-rail, but in the early 18th century a single, central splat, shaped somewhat like a vase or a fiddle, extended the full length of the back and, on good examples, was attached to the

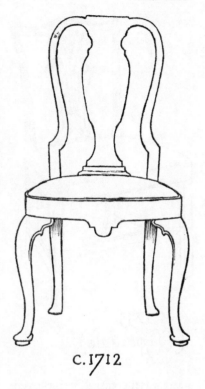

c. 1712

seat-rail by means of a shoe-piece (*q.v.*). This form of construction persisted into the third quarter of the century.

The paw foot (*q.v.*) appeared in the 1720s but was more frequent after 1730, the cabriole legs to which it formed a terminal being often heavy and over-elaborate in treatment, while contemporary armchairs sometimes had vicious-looking eagles' heads at the ends of the arms. During this phase, maho-

39

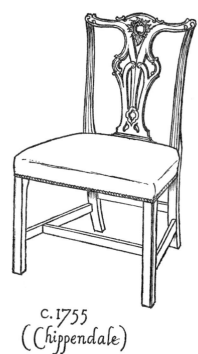

c. 1755
(Chippendale)

ance, and noticeable variations in size began to occur due to the practice of regulating the scale according to that of the rooms in which chairs were intended to be placed. Chinese and 'Gothick' motifs were employed as well as rococo, which was known at the time as the 'modern style', and at the same time the front legs of chairs were often of square section with the inner angle chamfered off. This type of leg was very

gany was increasingly employed as an alternative to walnut, designs, however, being identical in both materials during the period of transition.

In about 1740, the essentials of what is usually known as the Chippendale style first manifested themselves. Matthias Lock (*q.v.*) published a book of rococo designs, and the erstwhile solid splat began to be fretted with involved strapwork patterns. Seats and backs took on a broad, square appear-

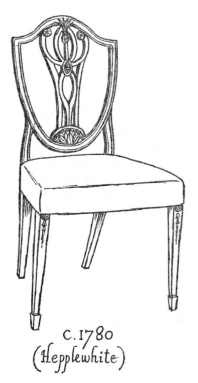

c. 1780
(Hepplewhite)

c. 1810
(Regency)

a spade (therm) foot (*q.v.*). Hepplewhite (*q.v.*) exhibited the prevailing taste in chairs in the *Guide*, published in 1788 two years after his death, by which time classical influence, while still in evidence, had become somewhat diluted.

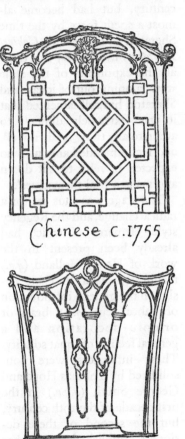

Chinese c. 1755

Gothic c. 1755

frequently used as an alternative to the cabriole until the last quarter of the 18th century.

In the 1760s, the neo-classical style, inaugurated chiefly by James Stuart and Robert Adam (*q.q.v.*), slowly commenced to influence the design and ornament of chairs although, as in the case of silverware, it was not generally adopted until about 1770. Backs were oval and, from about 1775, of shield-shape, while legs tapered downwards and often terminated in

Sheraton (*q.v.*) showed many chairs with square backs in the *Drawing Book*, which formed an apt record of taste in the last decade of the 18th century. The slim elegance of the neo-classical style was carried over into the early years of the new century, but had become almost a spent force by the time Sheraton published his *Cabinet Dictionary* in 1803. By this time, all the exponents of the style were running out of ideas, and Sheraton himself lamented that it was 'extremely difficult to attain to any thing really novel', and recommended anyone who expected novelty to 'sit down and make a trial themselves'.

The stage was thus set for a radical change, and the Regency style, elements of which had already been present in the work of Henry Holland (*q.v.*) manifested itself in chair design in the general introduction of 'sabre' legs (*q.v.*), brass or ormolu decoration and a general feeling of squat solidity. These influences were consolidated by Thomas Hope and George Smith (*q.q.v.*) in the first decade of the 19th century, but the second of these designers published a further work in 1826 from which it is evident that the prevailing taste

C.1790

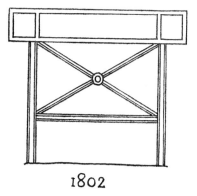

1802

for massiveness contained the seeds of a decadence which was to make the degeneracy of the Victorian era inevitable.

Chair-Table: see Table-Chair.

Chaise Longue: a French term (long chair) in vogue from the second half of the 18th century, denoting an upholstered day-bed or couch.

Thomas Sheraton described their use as 'to rest or loll upon after dinner'.

Chamber Horse: a contrivance for providing indoor exercise introduced in about 1760, and persisting into the 19th century. It consisted of a chair with arms or vertical posts and seat like a concertina set on end which permitted an up and down movement.

Chambers, Sir William: celebrated architect, his knighthood was conferred upon him by the King of Sweden, but he was permitted to use it in England by George III. He visited China, and issued *Designs for Chinese Buildings and Furniture* in 1757, though he left no doubt that he considered the Chinese manner inferior to the styles of classical antiquity and unsuitable to the British climate. He designed some important furniture for Blenheim Palace.

Chamfer: a bevelled or canted edge formed by shaving off a right-angle; usually found on the inner angles of the straight front legs of certain chairs from about 1740, and much used in the Chippendale period.

Cheese Coaster: a trough-shaped object about 18 in. long on a rectangular base mounted on small castors, used to facilitate the circulation of a cheese or part of one round the dining-table. Cheese coasters first appeared in the last quarter of the 18th century and were usually in polished mahogany.

Chest or Coffer: the most widely-distributed early item of furniture in the middle ages and of which examples have survived in England from the 13th century onwards. Primitive specimens were made by hollowing out a section of tree-trunk, a slice cut off the top serving as a lid; this method

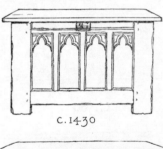

c. 1430

c. 1530

of construction is still enshrined in the word 'trunk' (French: *tronc*). Until about 1300 chests tended to be of massive oak, either plain or decorated with chip-carved roundels and/or Gothic arcading, and often painted in bright colours. Carved ornament followed the prevailing architectural mode: decorated Gothic until the late 14th century overlapping perpendicular Gothic, which continued into the early 16th century, modified latterly by the presence of the depressed Tudor arch. Linenfold (*q.v.*) panelling was introduced from the duchy of Burgundy in the late 15th century and was even more pre-

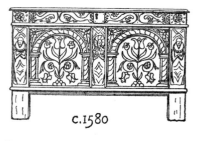

c.1580

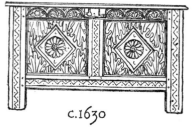

c.1630

valent after 1500. It remained popular after the introduction of Italian-inspired motifs such as Romayne heads (*q.v.*), foliate scrollwork, guilloche (*q.v.*), round-headed arches and other renaissance elements. From the middle of the 16th century inlay was employed, the woods used being chiefly holly for light parts and bog oak which was almost black. At this period, and in the very early 17th century, stiles and muntins (*q.q.v.*) were occasionally in the form of grotesque demi-figures with pointed beards and sometimes female breasts as well. Similar ornament appeared on the heads of beds. Greater restraint gradually supervened in the 17th century and although carving was often rich, it was generally simplified, making more use of foliage such as formalised acanthus leaves, while lozenge or diamond-shaped motifs became especially prevalent and were frequently the only surface ornament. From the early 17th century, the interiors of chests were increasingly provided with candle-boxes spanning one end.

Chests were not confined to the age of oak. In the late 17th century sophisticated examples veneered with walnut and decorated with floral marquetry continued the ancient tradition, to be followed by chests, on various kinds of stands, constructed of Chinese lacquer panels or japanned in England with decoration of Chinese type. During the currency of the style associated with the name of William Kent, elaborate chests, often of sarcophagus form, were decorated with gilt gesso of great richness. They belong, in general, to the period 1720–1740, after which the incidence of chests declined, though some were designed and made in carved mahogany. Chippendale illustrated a few designs for 'cloths chests', but such objects never achieved any considerable popularity in the 18th century owing to their inconvenience compared with chests of drawers.

Chest of Drawers: the basic principle of the chest of drawers began to emerge in the second half of the 16th century when oak chests with hinged lids were sometimes made with a drawer or drawers in the base, but the principle was not developed further until the middle of the 17th century. Hybrid pieces then began to appear either with drawers concealed behind cupboard doors or with some drawers visible and others enclosed, while a relationship with the ordinary chest or coffer was often preserved by a hinged lid on top, covering a shallow recess.

Orthodox chests of drawers in oak were made soon after 1660, typically with raised polygonal panels on the fronts sometimes inlaid with various woods and bone. In addition to examples of normal size some, in two unequal stages, were the ancestors of the later tallboys (*q.v.*), while others were mounted on stands. The latter continued to be made in the early 18th century. In about 1680 appeared a more sophisticated version with graduated drawers, its elegant proportions remaining more or less standard throughout the Georgian era. Many had bracket feet of fully-developed type, though ball feet continued to be used as well. The best examples were veneered with walnut, but other woods such as yew were also employed. When decoration occurred, it often took the form of floral marquetry contained in reserves, with 'seaweed' marquetry following at the end of the century. Japanning was also used, and oyster veneers (*q.v.*) remained prevalent for some time after 1700. Initially, many of these chests had no handles on the drawers, which had to be opened by pulling on the key, but the inconvenience of this arrangement, with attendant risk of damage, soon became apparent, and single-drop handles of brass or even engraved silver were quickly introduced, followed by drop-handles of loop form which swung freely from two pivots. The latter type remained in use throughout the 18th century, but in the Adam period was superseded in popular esteem by ring-handles with circular, and later, oval, escutcheon plates deriving from classical paterae (*q.v.*).

Chests of drawers were made in greater numbers after the general adoption of mahogany, some of them being of an elaborate and sumptuous appearance which brings them into the category of commodes (*q.v.*). Bow-fronted chests were introduced in the last quarter of the 18th century, and Sheraton devised a contrary form with concave front, of which examples have survived. Writing facilities were embodied in some chests of drawers from the Queen Anne period. These mostly took the form of a pull-out slide just below the top or a top which folded over and rested on runners (see Bachelor's Chest), while in the second half of the 18th century a writing surface was sometimes provided inside the top drawer.

Chest-upon-Chest: see Tallboy.

Cheval Glass or Mirror: an innovation of the late 18th century, when it was called a Horse Dressing Glass, comprising a tall toilet mirror swinging between two uprights or sliding up and down supported by concealed weights as in a sash window. The early name probably derives from the two pairs of splayed legs which were somewhat suggestive of the contemporary representation of a horse at full stretch.

Cheveret or Sheveret: a name used by Gillow's of Lancaster in the late 18th century to describe a miniature writing-table with tapering legs and a drawer in the frieze, surmounted by a removable stand, for books, correspondence, etc., spanned

46

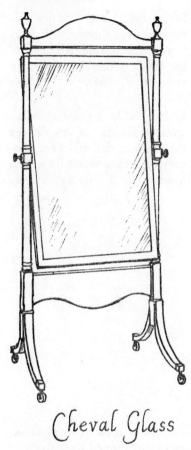

Cheval Glass

Cheveret

Chiffonier: a term of French origin with several meanings. In 18th-century France it denoted a tall chest of drawers, and is still used in this sense in the United States. The earliest English variant, which appeared in the mid-18th century, derived from the *chiffonière*, a low chest on legs, sometimes with writing facilities. In the early 19th century the term was

by a curved carrying handle, sometimes with drawers below. The writing surface is disclosed by pulling out the drawer in the frieze. They were made in mahogany but more frequently in satinwood. Designs varied in detail and sometimes included a platform between the legs.

47

applied to a small cupboard containing shelves for books, often surmounted by a platform supported on pillars, and this is the commonest surviving type. At the end of the 18th century Henry Holland, who carried out some alterations at Carlton House for the Prince of Wales, designed a large chiffonier in rosewood with bookshelves in the centre, flanked by open, quadrant-shaped shelves at the ends, with a smaller set of bookshelves on top. It was clearly under French influence.

Chimney Glass: otherwise known as an overmantel mirror, the chimney glass first appeared in the late 17th century and usually consisted of a large central plate with a smaller one each side. They were made throughout the 18th century in all the succeeding decorative styles, baroque, rococo, neoclassical, etc., and were usually very tall. In about 1800, there was a general reversion to the original 17th-century horizontal shape, with the divisions between the plates covered by gilt fillets in keeping with the frame, and often with a row of gilt balls under the cornice. The most popular type of the early 19th century had a deep

frieze below the cornice decorated in gilt gesso with Ares in a car drawn by lions, trumpeting angels overhead and Charity relieving Poverty.

China Table: a name given to various kinds of small tea tables from the mid-18th century, at a time when there was a widespread interest in cera-

China Table

mics. The tops of these tables were surrounded by pierced or solid galleries to safeguard the china. There is a modern tendency to describe them as 'silver tables', but this usage seems without warrant and has probably arisen from a misinterpretation of the common 18th-century description of large silver salvers as 'tables'. See Tea Table.

Chinoiserie: otherwise known as the Chinese Taste, began to exert some slight influence in the late 16th century, reinforced later by importations of the East India Company, but dating effectively from about 1660 when the traffic increased and aroused widespread enthusiam. Interest waxed and waned throughout the 18th century and finally died out after 1800. Chippendale made particularly effective use of 'Chinese' motifs combined with rococo (*q.v.*), and imported Chinese panels were often embodied in commodes in the second half of the 18th century. These panels were sometimes made in England by cutting down Chinese screens, often with scant regard for the original composition.

Chintz: painted or printed calico began to be imported from the Orient by the East India Company in the second quarter of the 17th century. In the reign of Charles II it was often the practice to import calico from the East with the designs drawn by hand; they were then coloured in England. Enthusiasm for chintz had reached such heights towards the end of Queen Anne's

reign that it was used for ladies' dresses, curtains and upholstery, but as great injury began to be suffered by the British textile industry, the traffic was forbidden by an Act of 1722, and the use of the fabric was banned. This restriction was lifted in 1774 in favour of chintz woven and printed in England, and Hepplewhite, in the *Guide* (1788) recommended it for bed-hangings.

Chip-Carving: a simple form of decoration virtually confined to oak furniture, involving the formation of shallow, gouged recesses in various patterns, beginning in the early 13th century in England and continuing effectively up to the late 17th century, especially in country districts. Occurring chiefly in the form of roundels in the early Gothic period, it continued later as ancillary ornament with the more sophisticated relief carving.

Chippendale, Thomas (1718–1779): designer and manufacturer, born at Otley, Yorkshire. He came to London at an unspecified date and is traced to Long Acre in 1749. He moved to Northumberland

49

Court (Somerset Court) in the Strand in 1752, and in 1753 occupied important premises in St. Martin's Lane, a cabinet-making quarter. Here, in 1754, he published *The Gentleman and Cabinet-Maker's Director*, a large folio of designs for furniture, with 160 illustrations engraved chiefly by his friend Matthew Darly after the rococo experts, Matthias Lock and Henry Copland, whom Chippendale employed but to whom he gave no credit, claiming the designs as his own.

Although the *Director* was the first comprehensive book of furniture designs ever to be published, the basic essentials of the 'Chippendale' style had already begun to appear in about 1740. In the *Director*, rococo (*q.v.*) motifs were mingled with 'Gothick' and Chinese, usually in very happy combination. It should be noted that Chippendale never once illustrated the claw-and-ball foot, which was quite outmoded on chairs by 1754, except here and there in the provinces where fashion lagged behind. Before the publication of his catalogue Chippendale was in no way celebrated and sprang into fame only as a result of the appearance of the

Director. He was able to finance the production of the book and his business with capital furnished by his partner, James Rannie, whose contribution seems to have been confined to administration. A second edition, similar to the first, appeared in 1755 to satisfy an enormous residual demand, and a third in 1762. By this time the rococo style was being superseded by the neo-classical, but Chippendale seemed unable to forget that he had been the chief official protagonist of rococo, and the 1762 edition of the *Director* paid merely perfunctory recognition to the new influence. Some of the designs consisted, in fact, of an incongruous mixture of the two styles, for example, a neo-classical sideboard-table with a large and obtrusive piece of asymmetrical rococo ornament forming an apron in the centre of the frieze.

About this time Robert Adam (*q.v.*) began to commission Chippendale to make furniture to his designs, and this is probably the best he ever produced. The collaboration between the two lasted until Chippendale's death. Rannie died in 1766, and in about 1771 Chippendale took into partnership one of his executives, Thomas Haig, the firm being known thereafter as Chippendale, Haig & Co. The *Director* was a great success, and its wide distribution resulted in an unprecedented measure of standardisation all over the British Isles, the designs for chairs, in which it excelled, being generally simplified in the provinces to suit the pockets of less wealthy purchasers and the lower standard of skill in carving of local craftsmen.

Other more famous cabinet-makers were working at the same time as Chippendale including William Vile (*q.v.*), and he did not carry out any work for the Royal household which was employing many other furniture-makers. It is only the publication of the *Director* which has caused Chippendale's name to become a generic term for a style which he did not initiate and of which he was not the most skilled exponent, though there is no doubt that his designs for chairs reached a high level of excellence. See Chairs and Commode.

Chippendale, Thomas, the Younger (1749–1822): succeeded to the partnership on

his father's death in 1779 and continued trading as Chippendale & Haig until Haig quitted the business in 1796. He was made bankrupt in 1804, but he evidently recovered from his difficulties in a short while. Some of his furniture has survived, that which he made in the early 19th century being elegant and lacking some of the less desirable excesses of the Regency period. He had a number of distinguished clients including Lord Harewood, the Earl of Pembroke and Sir Richard Hoare of Stourhead in Wiltshire.

Clap Table: see Console Table.

Claw-and-Ball Foot: of ancient Chinese origin comprising, in Britain and British spheres of influence, a ball gripped by four talons. It had occurred on English silverware in the 16th century, but was popular on cabriole legs of furniture chiefly between 1710 and 1740, though it continued long after this on the legs of dumb waiters, tripod tables and side tables, and remained fashionable in provincial centres and the American colonies after it had become outmoded in London. It was in no way characteristic of the Chippendale style, as is sometimes supposed.

Claw Table: an 18th-century term for a small table supported on a central pillar with three, or occasionally four, splayed legs attached to the base. The common tripod table is a familiar example.

Clay's Ware: a kind of papier-mâché patented by Henry Clay in 1772, often brilliantly japanned and decorated with Wedgwood cameos. He made all kinds of furniture, tea-caddies, etc., and did a thriving trade in tea-trays.

Clothes Press: clothes were generally stored in chests from the middle ages until the 18th century, but although tall oak presses in which clothes could be hung were known in the 17th century, from which a number has survived, they did not begin to be fashionable until the last quarter of the century following. Meanwhile, clothes-presses achieved growing popularity from the 1740s, some of the earliest being mounted on separate stands with paw feet. A two-stage variety was introduced soon

after, the lower part consisting of a chest of drawers of varying height supporting a press, enclosed by two doors, containing pull-out shelves or trays. These slid on runners applied to the inner sides of the carcase or in grooves cut in the thickness of the wood. The door-panels were sometimes made from single planks of mahogany. Examples were illustrated by Chippendale in the *Director* and by Hepplewhite in the *Guide*, the latter showing a type with oval, recessed panels in the doors which gained considerable popularity.

A design in Sheraton's *Drawing Book* was probably responsible for the increasing recognition of the hanging wardrobe. This was a composite piece consisting of a normal two-stage clothes-press with a narrow wing on each side equipped with hangers sliding on metal rods, and providing uninterrupted space for even the longest garment. The older type of clothes-press with sliding shelves continued to be made in the Victorian period, and is now often described by the modern jargon phrase 'gentleman's wardrobe', possibly because it is of very little use to ladies even with the shelves removed and a rod for hangers fitted inside.

Club Foot: a terminal to a straight or cabriole leg shaped somewhat like a golf club, of outward-curving, flattened spherical form, common from about 1705 until the late 18th century.

Cobb, John: see Vile, William.

Cock Beading: a narrow projecting moulding of semicircular section, applied to the edges of drawers from about 1720 onwards.

Cock-Fighting Chair: a modern jargon term sometimes applied to reading chairs (*q.v.*) which could be sat upon astride, facing the back, as well as in the orthodox manner. No chair was ever specifically made for cock-fighting and this term should not be used.

Cock's Head Hinge: a plate hinge with four curving extensions pierced for nails, arranged symmetrically in pairs on either side of the central barrel, occurring mainly on oak furniture of the 17th century. The extensions terminate in finials more or less suggestive

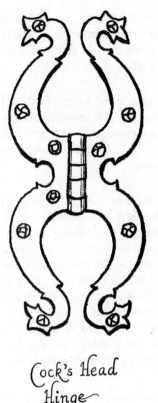

Cock's Head Hinge

of cocks' heads. These hinges developed from a 16th-century prototype with the finials treated more simply.

Coffer: a term which, in a practical sense, it is no longer possible to distinguish from 'chest' (*q.v.*), as it has signified

53

different things at different times and has been used loosely for centuries. It derives from the French *coffre*.

Coin: a word sometimes used in the 18th century to indicate a corner cupboard, and deriving from the French word *encoignure*.

Colonnette: a small column; often used in connection with furniture to denote in particular a pilaster (*q.v.*) of almost completely circular section, applied to the front of a piece of case-furniture and extended downwards below the base to form a short leg. Colonnettes were used chiefly in the late 18th and early 19th centuries.

Comb-Back Chair: a term of fairly recent origin describing a kind of Windsor chair (*q.v.*) with a higher cresting at the back raised on sticks prolonged above the main hoop and somewhat suggestive of a hair-comb.

Commode: a term of uncertain application even in France where it originated, but used from the early 18th century, and from about 1730 in Eng-

land, to denote a sumptuous chest of drawers or a cupboard of similar proportions enclosing drawers or shelves. Early English examples were monumental but inelegant, despite the excellence of the materials and the superb workmanship of makers such as William Vile, but became more graceful during the rococo period, a number being illustrated by Chippendale in the *Director*. The outline of the front was

Commode c.1755
(Chippendale)

generally conditioned by the profile of the contemporary cabriole leg, but straight-sided versions, often of D-section, became popular in the second half of the 18th century. These were often decorated with Chinese panels, neo-classical motifs and oval or circular medallions containing painted compositions after such artists as Angelica Kauffmann, Pergolesi, Cipriani and Zucchi. Pilasters in the form of colonnettes (*q.v.*) usually reeded, appeared at the end of the 18th century and continued after 1800, when commodes fell into a decline. Their function was chiefly ostentatious and they were mainly sited in reception-rooms though a few, with dressing-table fitments in the top drawer, sometimes occurred in the bedrooms of the wealthy. In the early 18th century they were sometimes called 'sideboards' and Chippendale called them 'commode tables', both terms indicating a preoccupation with the top surface. It is evident that, in the last decade of the 18th century, they had entirely abandoned any pretence they may have had previously to serve as functional receptacles, for Thomas Sheraton commented: 'these pieces of furniture are never intended for use but for ornament'. The word *commode* is now the normal French term for a chest of drawers, and it was not until the Victorian period that it was used in England to denote a close-stool. Georgians would have found this usage ludicrous and incomprehensible.

Confidante: a type of late 18th-century sofa, illustrated by Robert Adam and George Hepplewhite, with an extra seat at each end facing out sideways.

Console: an architectural term of French origin signifying a bracket, usually scroll-shaped, supporting a projection above it, and applied also to furniture. In this connection they began to be used from the second half of the 16th century, when they sometimes occurred on the friezes of oak tables, ostensibly supporting the projecting edge of the top. They continued to be used into the 19th century.

Console Table: a side table which leans against a wall, the outer side being supported by inward-curving legs or a carved figure such as an eagle standing on a wide plinth. Console tables were introduced into England from France in the early 18th century, when they were given the inelegant name of 'clap tables', either because they were clapped up against the wall, or because they leaned against the clap-board which formed the panelling. The tops were of wood, marble or scagliola (*q.v.*). The term is sometimes extended to similar tables with vertical supports on the wall-side also.

Convex Mirror: a looking glass with an outward-bulging surface and of circular shape. These mirrors were evidently known to some extent in the medieval period, for the early 15th-century portrait by Jan van Eyck of Giovanni Arnolfini and his wife, in the National Gallery, London, shows one at the far end of the room, reflecting the entire scene in miniature. From about 1800 convex mirrors began to be made in large numbers and continued popular throughout the Regency period. The gilt frames were sometimes fairly plain, but were often decorated with carved foliage and surmounted by an eagle, usually with small gilt balls suspended from its beak by thin chains.

Convex Moulding: a moulding shaped like part of the circumference of a circle, often occurring in the form of a frieze just below the horizontal cornices of chests on stands, scrutoirs (*q.v.*), etc., of the late 17th century, and sometimes described otherwise by the architectural term 'torus'. These

friezes usually contained a long, shallow drawer.

Copland, Henry: an early and skilled exponent of the rococo style, published plates of rococo ornament in 1746; with Mathias Lock (*q.v.*) was responsible for many of the furniture designs in Chippendale's *Director*.

Cornice: an architectural term signifying the projecting top moulding of the entablature of a building and the analogous portion of a cabinet; applied also in the 17th and 18th centuries to the wooden screening from behind which window and bed curtains were suspended.

Corner Cupboard: a cupboard designed to fit into a corner of a room, with a straight or curved front and usually furnished with shelves; known in the reign of Charles I (1625–1649) but rare until the last decade of the 17th century when such pieces suddenly came into fashion for the storage of china. The earliest were hung on the wall, and this type continued to the end of the 18th century, but in about 1700 the standing variety, sometimes known as a 'corner cabinet', with a base resting on the floor, was introduced, and was made until about 1800 though to a less extent than the hanging type. In the middle of the 18th century a version known in France as an *encoignure*, and in England as a 'coin' or 'ecoineur' superseded the existing types in fashionable esteem. It was mounted on legs in the various contemporary styles, and contained graduated shelves, and was the kind more likely to be encountered in a wealthy household than its predecessors, which continued, nevertheless, to be made in large numbers for those in middling or modest circumstances. Decoration, when it was present at all, accorded with the prevailing mode. In the late 18th century, for example, fronts were usually curved like those of bow-fronted chests of drawers, and were embellished with neo-classical ornament and a motif which was very popular at the period consisting of a large inlaid whelk-shell, which often occurred on the falls of bureaux, tea-trays, etc. This motif was much used again in the early years of the 20th century, some of the objects to which it was

applied being well-made and already developing some appearance of antiquity.

Coromandel Wood: Bombay ebony from the Coromandel coast of India. Sheraton described it as resembling black rosewood but intermingled with light stripes. It was extensively used for banding in the Regency period, and some pieces such as card tables were often veneered with it all over.

Court Cupboard: a much mis-used term which is applied correctly only to unenclosed structures, usually in three tiers,

Court Cupboard c.1600

common from the middle ages until the 17th century, and used to display drinking vessels and vessels connected with the serving of wine and ale. The word 'court' comes from the French *court*—short, while a 'cup board' was an open arrangement of boards or shelves for cups, etc. Quite early, a small storage area enclosed by hinged doors and known as an aumbry (*q.v.*) was introduced, and in the 17th century the term 'cupboard' began to be employed in its corrupt modern sense. See Press Cupboard.

Credence: (*a*) a small side-table, wider at the back than the front, with a cupboard in the upper half, used in churches to contain the reserved sacrament; from Latin *credere*—to believe; (*b*) a similar structure, of which oak examples have survived in England from the 16th century, probably owing its name to the fact that a trusted servant would stand at it to sample his master's food and drink as a precaution against poisoning. The term has been extended to all splay-fronted oak pieces of a similar kind used for serving and storage in ordinary domestic surroundings. These achieved

Credence c.1640

some popularity in the first half of the 17th century and most surviving specimens are of this period. The legs below the enclosed upper portion were united by stretchers which were sometimes covered by a pot-board to enhance the utility of the piece.

Cresting: the ornament surmounting mirrors, cabinets, picture-frames, chair-backs, etc.

Croft: a small filing-cabinet with a writing surface in the top drawer; named after Sir Herbert Croft, the lexicographer, who commissioned one in the late 18th century for the orderly storage of papers.

Cross-Banding: a banding of veneer, on or near the border of a surface, with the grain of the wood at right-angles to the band; first used on drawer-fronts in the reign of Charles II (1660–1685) and current throughout the entire Georgian period.

Cross-Rail: a rail running horizontally across the back of a chair as distinct from a splat or splad (*q.v.*).

Cupboard: originally an open arrangement of boards or shelves for displaying cups, etc., during a meal, common from the middle ages to the 17th century. Part of the structure was sometimes enclosed behind a hinged door or doors, and the word became transferred to this portion in the early 17th century, thus attaining its present significance.

Cup Turning, Inverted Cup Turning: a turned moulding, shaped somewhat like a goblet, found throughout the mahogany period on appropriate parts of furniture such as bedposts and the pillars of tripod tables. The design had occurred earlier, in a more strongly-emphasised form, on

Cylinder Desk

legged furniture from 1690 to about 1700, when it was shaped like an inverted goblet with hemispherical bowl.

Curul or Curricule Chair: a name given by Sheraton in 1803 to a chair in the classical style having a long seat and a low, tub-shaped back; probably inspired by a light horse-drawn vehicle with the same name.

Cylinder Desk: a writing table introduced in the late 18th century, sometimes set over a chest of drawers or cupboards like a bureau, sometimes raised on legs or end-standards. The top was enclosed either by a curved panel consisting of a quarter cylinder or a tambour (*q.v.*) of the same shape; the forerunner of the roll-top desk.

Cypress: a wood indigenous to certain Levantine countries which became naturalised in England and Europe, used from the middle ages for boxes and chests, and esteemed for its resistance to woodworm and rot.

D

Darly, Matthew (Mathias): printseller, designer, caricaturist and engraver, chiefly celebrated as the engraver of most of the plates in *The Gentleman and Cabinet-Maker's Director*, by his friend Thomas Chippendale. Darly published several books of designs, particularly in the Chinese taste, and *The Compleat Architect* (1770).

Davenport: a narrow writing-desk with sloping top and drawers beneath mounted either on short legs or a plinth, probably named after a certain Captain Davenport for whom Gillow's of Lancaster made a desk in the late 18th century. All show a general similarity of proportion and appearance, but often differ in detail. In some, the top can be slid forward so that the user's legs may be accommodated underneath the projection, in others, the top projects permanently and is supported on cylindrical columns. The drawers are usually at the side so that they can be reached when

the desk is in use. Survivors are numerous from the Victorian period, when they were mostly made of walnut, the projecting front supported on exaggerated cabriole legs of pronounced ogee-form.

Day-Bed: introduced in the early 16th century and used for sitting or reclining on during the day. Day-beds were very popular in the second half of the 17th century and continued throughout the century following. Day-beds are distinguished from settees and sofas by the fact that they are in the form of a wide chair elongated to the length of an adult's body and open along the sides. In the second half of the 18th century they appeared in the more sophisticated guise of the *chaise longue*.

Deal: originally, a deal was a wooden board, usually of pine or fir, not over 3 in. thick but over 9 in. wide. These boards were commonly imported from the Baltic region. By the late

16th century the term was beginning to denote the actual timber. In the second half of the 18th century, when it became the almost invariable practice to paint wall-panelling, deal superseded oak, as the knots and imperfections of the wood were concealed. It was used as a cheaper alternative to oak for veneered work from the late 17th century.

Dentil Moulding: an architectural term denoting a moulding below a cornice or pediment of a building or piece of case furniture consisting of a row of small cubes suggestive of blunt teeth; much used in the mahogany period.

Derbyshire Chair: also known as a Yorkshire-Derbyshire chair; a mid-17th century armless chair (backstool) of oak, made with two main types of back: (*a*) with arcading between the uprights resting on a cross-rail with a space below, and (*b*) with two large, arched cross-rails decorated with carving and with two inward-curving points below each reminiscent of crabs' claws. Both types were decorated with small stuck-in bobbins and the uprights generally terminated

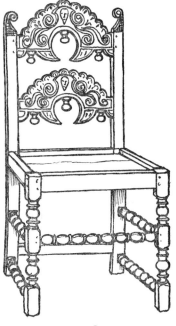

Derbyshire Chair

in volutes facing outward or inward. The wooden seats were usually dished for squab cushions.

Derbyshire Desk: a popular name, probably inaccurate, for small, portable writing-boxes with sloping lids and often carved, made all over Britain in the 17th century. See also Bible Box.

Deuddarn: a Welsh press-cupboard (*q.v.*) in two stages.

Diamond Ornament: see Lozenge.

Dining-Tables: from the early Gothic period until the beginning of the 16th century, tables used for main meals consisted almost invariably of long rectangular tops resting on trestles of various kinds: an arrangement which enabled them to be dismantled after meals and stowed out of the way. Smaller tables of circular or polygonal shape, sometimes mounted on central pillars, are occasionally to be seen in medieval manuscript illustrations, but it is often evident from accompanying details that their use was generally confined to breakfast. Large tables of fixed construction, known as 'dormant tables', were in existence but were exceedingly rare, and references to trestle tables occurred even in the reign of Henry VIII (1509–1547), but fixed tables were being made in increasing numbers and soon became standard in normal households. They were usually made of oak like other furniture of the period, and the legs, which varied in number according to the length of the top, were generally of square section, with the angles bevelled, and were all united by stretchers slightly above floor-level. Some affinity with Tudor architecture was sometimes displayed by a depressed Gothic arch in each of the rails, but the majority were evidently plain and unadorned. Draw tables (*q.v.*) were introduced at this period and were identical in stylistic details.

In the second half of the 16th century the legs of large tables were, like bed-posts and the front supports of court cupboards (*q.v.*), commonly embellished with bold, turned protuberances somewhat suggestive of covered urns, and the tops of the legs often terminated in Ionic capitals which entirely failed to give such furniture a convincing classical flavour. Carved ornament was practically universal and often took the form of radial gadroons (*q.v.*) on the covers of the urns, vertical flutes and/or gadroons elsewhere and large acanthus leaves, while the rails might be covered with vine-trails or rows of contiguous lunettes (*q.v.*), though the latter were commoner in the Jacobean period. Very occasionally, tables of the Elizabethan era (1558–1603) were equipped with hinges at each corner of the frame so that they could be folded up for transport.

No immediate changes occurred in the early 17th century, but there was a growing tendency for the bulges to become narrower; they were soon replaced altogether by balusters, plain cylinders and other forms of a less pronounced character than formerly.

Large joined tables of traditional form continued to be made after 1660 when oval gate-leg tables (*q.v.*) had begun to usurp their function in fashionable surroundings, and some which have survived in country places even bear dates in the first half of the 18th century. In general, however, they fell out of favour. Despite the adoption of walnut by cabinet-makers for case-furniture and chairs, most gate-leg tables were made entirely of oak, though a few had legs of solid walnut and even fewer had walnut tops as well. They persisted into the 18th century with very little change and are consequently difficult to date with any accuracy. More certainly of the Queen Anne period was a kind of table whose prototype, in massive oak, had occurred sparsely in the 17th century. It was made

in two semicircular halves which were fitted together for dining; the walnut used in its construction and the cabriole legs betray its early 18th-century origin.

With the introduction of mahogany, many dining-tables had large hinged flaps which sometimes almost reached the floor. They were supported in a horizontal position by swinging out one of the legs on each side of the fixed central portion. The tops were then either oval, circular or rectangular and were often of large size, while the rectangular ones were sometimes supplied in pairs so that they could be placed together to provide an increased surface area.

Considering the importance in a household of a table at which formal meals were taken, with all the accompanying costly elegances in the form of silver candlesticks or candelabra and centre-pieces, not to mention the salts, cruet-frames, flatware, etc., it seems surprising that Chippendale should have made no mention of dining-tables in the *Director*, though they were often referred to in contemporary invoices. The fact is that they were not conceived as permanent entities, for neither manufacturers nor purchasers seemed able to abandon the idea that they should consist of *ad hoc* assemblies of various portions which could be separated when not required for a meal. The common D-shaped ends, for example, were placed against the wall as side-tables, and these have often become dissociated from the other elements with which they once formed complete garnitures. Even as late as 1791 there was a reference to 'a set of Mahogany dining Tables, consisting of one square frame with 2 flaps and 2 round ends with a flap to each ... the whole or any part to Join together at pleasure', but at about this time a new conception began to emerge.

This was the familiar and much-reproduced type of dining-table mounted on upwards of two pillar-and-claw supports which offered no impediment to the legs of the diners. The permanent central portion was divisible centrally across the width and, when pulled apart, an unsupported leaf could be fixed in the resultant space or any number of rectangular tops, each with its own pillar-and-claw. Some of these tables, with a large number of

additional sections, were of immense length. There was some variation in the design of the supports. A few consisted of baluster-shaped pillars with four splayed cabriole legs attached to the base of each. Others comprised four slender columns resting on a flat platform with a downward-curving leg at each corner. The majority, however, had thick, cylindrical shafts with four square-section, concave legs which were sometimes reeded on the upper surfaces. Each leg had a castor attached beneath a square brass socket.

This type continued into the 19th century with unabated popularity, the edges of the tops being reeded more frequently than in the late 18th century, but changes occurred in the supports, which lost their original elegant simplicity. The pillars tended to be embellished with elaborate turnings, while the claw legs developed projections suggestive of noses or beaks near the point where they joined the pillar. Castors were often attached to sockets shaped like lions' paws.

In 1800, Richard Gillow (*q.v.*) invented a telescopic dining-table with normal vertical legs.

The same device had been used on rare occasions in connection with card tables of the mid-18th century, but Gillow was the first to apply the principal to dining-tables. Just before 1820 straight legs began to regain their former popularity as in the case of chairs, and might have vertical or spiral reeding, like certain tables of the Sheraton (*q.v.*) period, or turned collars which increased in number as the Regency era drew towards its close.

Smaller, circular dining-tables on central pillars had appeared shortly after 1800, and these achieved considerable popularity in surroundings where space was a consideration. Many had triangular bases with concave sides, terminating in large paw feet of a type popularised by Thomas Hope (*q.v.*). Some were in mahogany, others were veneered with rosewood, and all might be decorated near the edges with brass inlay like much other contemporary furniture of all kinds.

Dogwood: an indigenous British tree furnishing a hard timber of orange colour, used for inlay in the 16th and 17th centuries.

Dole Cupboard: a general term for a food cupboard, either standing or hanging, used in homes for the storage of food and in churches to contain bread for charitable distribution. All were pierced in various ways to permit the circulation of air, and were common from the middle ages until the end of the 17th century.

Dosser: a medieval term applied to the wall-hangings behind a seat, and sometimes, apparently, to a cushion on the back of a settle, etc., deriving from the French *dos*—the back.

Double Chest of Drawers: see Tallboy.

Dovetailing: a method of attaching adjacent sides of drawers and the carcases of case furniture, the name deriving from the shape of the interlocking protuberances at the angles. The through-dovetail was used from the middle ages until about 1700, when the stopped-dovetail was introduced. In the second, the dovetails appeared on the surface only on a side which was normally concealed or was not intended to be veneered, as it was found that veneer adhered better to a homogeneous surface.

Dowel: a cylindrical wooden pin, known also as a trenail, used for fixing parts of a piece of furniture together.

Dower Chest: a popular term which is not recommended owing to its lack of precision, indicating a chest of any description used primarily to contain the trousseau of a future bride. No special sort of chest was ever made for this purpose.

Draw Table: known also as a Draw-Leaf Table; a table with an extra leaf at each end, concealed beneath the top when closed, but which could be drawn out on runners, working through slots in the end rails, so that the table could be made almost double its normal length. Draw tables were made in England from the first half of the 16th century and for most of the 17th century.

Drawer Runners: rectangular-section strips of oak fixed on the inside of the carcases of chests of drawers in the 17th century and coinciding with grooves on the sides of the

drawers. This method of construction obviated wear on the bases of the drawers, and has returned to favour in modern times.

Dresser: a term in use from the middle ages, sometimes used as a synonym for 'cupboard' in its original sense. Cupboards, however, were devoted primarily to the display of plate, whereas the dresser was used for serving food. In the early 17th century the dresser became a distinct object. Initially, such pieces had drawers and cupboards below, reaching down to the floor, but in the second half of the century they were usually mounted on legs. From the latter part of the 17th century they were occasionally provided with shelved superstructures for the display of china, and this type continued through the 18th century. It was probably introduced from the Netherlands, but is now generally known as a Welsh dresser.

Dressing-Chest: a chest of drawers with a folding mirror and other conveniences in the top drawer, mostly in mahogany and dating from after 1760.

Dressing-Table: the earliest surviving dressing-tables date from the second half of the 17th century. These were a variety of small oak side-table, with one or two drawers in the frieze, and could be used for other purposes also. From the end of the 17th century these tables had either legs or two pedestals with a knee-hole between. They were often used for writing but could be rendered more convenient for toilet use by being sited beneath a looking-glass on the wall or having a toilet mirror (*q.v.*) stood on the top. These early types continued, with various modifications, throughout the Georgian period, but more elaborate examples began to be produced in the second quarter of the 18th century. Designs, which were often extremely ingenious, showed much variation, but all were furnished with mirrors, either permanently displayed or concealed beneath hinged tops or in drawers, and with small compartments for cosmetics, etc. Many embodied writing facilities and they were sometimes combined with bookcases.

Drop Handle: a term applied both to the brass, single-lobe drawer handles of the late 17th and early 18th centuries which were something like drops of liquid, and to the brass loop handles which dropped after being released, introduced in the late 17th century and continuing to be used thereafter despite the later introduction of other types.

Drop-In Seat: a removable, upholstered chair seat which rested on a narrow ledge within the seat rails, current from about 1700; sometimes called a Trap Seat.

Drop-Leaf Table: a table having one or two hinged flaps which can be permitted to hang down or be raised and supported by swung-out legs or brackets. The term is often restricted to tables other than gate-leg or Pembroke tables (*q.q.v.*) to avoid confusion.

Drum Table: a modern descriptive term applied to a circular library table, of varying size, having a frieze containing drawers and suggestive of a shallow drum. Such tables, which were often mounted on pillar-and-claw supports, were fashionable in the late 18th and early 19th centuries, though

Drum Table C. 1810

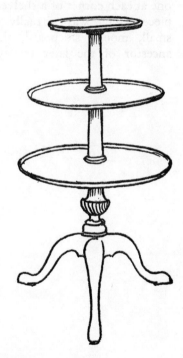

Dumb Waiter

in 1727; consisted of tiers of diminishing trays, usually circular and two to four in number, mounted one above the other on a central pillar or pillars and often capable of being rotated. The lowest section of the pillar rested on a base which was commonly of tripod form. Probably even the earliest were of mahogany, as it was desirable that the trays they never ousted the earlier two-pedestal type. In the Regency period they sometimes had hocked animal legs, each surmounted by a lion's head, linked at the base by a platform with concave sides between the feet.

Duchesse: a kind of couch, introduced in about 1780 and mentioned by both Hepplewhite and Sheraton (*q.v.*), consisting, either actually or ostensibly, of two tub-shaped or bergère armchairs linked by a long stool, and displaying the neo-classical taste.

Dumb Waiter: an English invention of about 1725, the first recorded reference to one being should be made from a single piece of wood, the planks afforded by the heart-wood of most walnut trees being too narrow for the purpose. Castors were sometimes used from about 1740. The tripod support was standard until 1800, but from the early Regency period four legs were often found, either of claw type, splaying out from the centre, or one at each corner of a shelved piece which was virtually a small, mobile sideboard, the ancestor of the later trolley.

Dumb waiters spread to the European continent in the second half of the 18th century. In England, two of them were commonly placed diagonally at opposite corners of the dining-table so that, as one diarist put it in 1784, 'conversation was not under any restraint by the servants being in the room'.

Dust Board: a thin wooden board between the drawers of a chest of drawers, introduced shortly after 1660.

E

Ebony: a generic term applied to hard, black woods, some of them not botanically related to true ebony. The latter is by no means always black. Ebony was extensively used as veneer on clock cases in the second half of the 17th century and occasionally on cabinets and tables, sometimes in association with applied silver ornament. During the Regency (*q.v.*) it was much favoured for inlay in the form of stringing, stars, etc.

Egg and Dart: sometimes called Egg and Tongue; a type of repeating architectural border ornament of classical origin used on furniture from the second half of the 16th century onward, and consisting of rows of ovolos with arrowheads between them. It is also sometimes known by the Latin name *Echinus*—a sea-urchin: a description which requires

Egg and Dart

some stretching of the imagination to reconcile with the appearance of the motif.

Egyptian Style: elements of the Egyptian taste, for example the anthemion (*q.v.*) were absorbed into ancient Greek art and into Roman art during the Empire when the cult of Isis was fashionable. In the English classical revival movement of the late 18th century, such elements were a mere surrogate of Graeco-Roman art and were used from this standpoint by, *inter alios*, Robert Adam, the sphinx, quite unlike Egyptian originals, being a familiar example. After the landing of Sir Ralph Abercromby at Aboukir in 1801, when the French army in Egypt was forced to capitulate, interest was suddenly stimulated, and this interest was further reinforced by the publication, shortly after 1802, of an English version of Denon's *Travels in Upper and Lower Egypt*, and by *Household Furniture and Interior Decoration* by Thomas Hope (1807), who had

71

studied Greek and Egyptian architecture in the late 18th century. These influences were responsible for the incidence in Regency design of various Egyptian details, notably, a tapering, rectangular-section pilaster in the form of a pedestal surmounted by an Egyptian head and with feet emerging from the base. These pedestals usually played a subordinate role as applied decoration, for example, at the sides of looking-glasses and cabinets, but were sometimes free-standing. Thomas Chippendale the younger (*q.v.*) used them effectively as the front legs of chairs in the early 19th century.

Elizabethan: an adjective pertaining to the reign of Queen Elizabeth I (1558–1603). Furniture of this era was mostly of oak and of heavy construction. Tables and bed-posts had large turned protuberances in the form of covered urns, and carved decoration, which was inclined to be lavish and sometimes overpowering, might comprise gadroons, round-headed arches, acanthus foliage, guilloche, vine-trails or lozenges (*q.q.v.*). Grotesque figures, often with pointed beards, were sometimes carved on the stiles and muntins (*q.v.*) of furniture of panelled construction. The style continued into the reign of James I (1603–1625) but gradually became more restrained. See Beds and Chests.

Elm: common elm has a strongly-marked grain but is difficult to work and liable to attack by woodworm, but country-made chairs of this wood have survived in comparatively large numbers from the 18th century. Wych elm is harder and with a more homogeneous grain, and was used in the 14th and 15th centuries for bows, as an alternative to yew. The seats of Windsor chairs were often made of this timber in the Georgian period. Burr-elm, in the form of veneer cut from the excrescences on tree trunks, was used in the early and late 18th century and the early 19th century.

Entablature: an architectural term indicating the topmost horizontal part of a building comprising architrave, frieze and cornice, found on furniture where appropriate from the renaissance onwards, and particularly marked in the time of William Kent (*q.v.*).

Escritoire: a writing cabinet of the late 17th century mounted on a stand or chest of drawers, and having a fall front supported in the horizontal position by chains or brass elbows. Contemporary names in England were Scriptor and Scrutoir. The type was succeeded by the more convenient bureau.

Escutcheon: a term deriving from the French *écu*—a shield, meaning a shield-shaped space for a coat of arms, crest, etc., and used in connection with furniture to denote a keyhole-plate of any shape, or a plate between a handle and a drawer-front.

Étagère: a 19th-century term for a small work-table with tiers of shelves below the top, and used later to confer greater dignity on the piece of furniture known otherwise as a What-not (*q.v.*). The use of this term is unnecesary.

F

Farthingale Chair: an armless, upholstered chair introduced in the early 17th century to accommodate ladies who wore the farthingale. This was a Spanish fashion which reached England in the late 16th century and consisted of a sort of cage-crinoline held out by whalebone, wire or cane, over a thick roll of cloth tied round the waist known as a 'bumroll'. Ladies wearing these objects were unable to get in between the arms of chairs—the queen of James I had one which was 4 ft. in diameter at the hips—and were accordingly obliged to sit on stools. The farthingale chair was responsible for a growing interest in upholstery, and many later chairs developed from the type after the farthingale itself went out of fashion in about 1625.

Farthingale Chair

Fiddle-Back: (*a*) a name used to describe the chair-splats of the early 18th century suggestive of a fiddle in shape; (*b*) mahogany sawn in such a manner that the grain contains flecks of pith similar to those in the sycamore often used for the backs of violins.

Fielded Panel: a bevel-edged panel with a surface level with the surrounding framework, occurring first on 17th-century drawer-fronts and later especially on the mahogany doors of clothes presses, wardrobes, etc., in the 18th century.

Fillet: a flat strip of wood occurring especially between flutes (q.v.) and deriving from Ionic and Corinthian columns.

Finial: a decorative projection surmounting a piece of furniture, for example, on the uprights of a chair-back, the cornice of a cabinet, etc.

Fire-Screen: a screen, often with a rushwork panel in the middle ages and with a needlework panel from about 1700. Eighteenth-century examples were generally adjustable, mounted on a pole with tripod base, or horse screens with four splayed legs. In the late 18th century they were sometimes covered with maps instead of needlework.

Flemish Scroll: a curving double scroll with one curve opposed to the other, occurring on the supports of tables in the late 17th century.

Flitcroft, Henry (1697–1769): architect and designer, first apprenticed to a joiner, his later career was due to the patronage of the Earl of Burlington; he became Clerk of the works and succeeded William Kent as Master Mason in 1748. He designed lavish furniture—some of which has survived—in the rich, contemporary style associated with the Palladian revival, making use of such elements as scallop shells, eagles' heads and scagliola (q.v.).

Flutes, Fluting: narrow, straight-sided vertical hollows deriving from classical columns and used as ornament on furniture from the renaissance, but especially in the 17th century and the late 18th century.

French Chairs: carved, high-backed upholstered armchairs in walnut or beech of the Charles II period, also mahogany chairs of the second half of the 18th century usually having cabriole legs and scroll feet, illustrated by both Chippendale and Hepplewhite.

French Polish: introduced into England in the 1820s and consisting of shellac dissolved in spirit rubbed on to the wood of furniture until the surface is glossy. Not only does French

Chippendale 'French' Chair

polish have a somewhat mere-tricious appearance, but it is easily damaged by heat and is less durable than the earlier polish obtained by working-in linseed, nut or poppy oil and beeswax, a method which is beneficial to the wood and produces a delightful patine or surface-quality.

Fretwork: the decorative piercing of parts of furniture especially popular in the Chippendale period and often found on the stretchers and sometimes the front legs of 'Chinese' and other chairs, sideboard tables, etc. The wooden galleries round the edges of some kettle-stands, tea-tables and dumb-waiter trays were generally built up from three thicknesses of mahogany veneer, glued together, which were then fretted. When similar designs are carved in low relief without piercing the result is usually known as Blind Fret.

Frieze: a horizontal band immediately below the cornice of a building or piece of furniture or the rail immediately below the top of a table.

G

Gadroons, Gadrooning: ornament consisting of convex lobes either straight or curved, sometimes alternating with flutes, occurring on the edges of parts of furniture notably from the 16th century to about the middle of the 18th century; also known as Nulling or Knurling.

Gadroons

'Games' Table c.1810

Gainsborough Chair: a modern jargon phrase applied to an 18th-century armchair with upholstered back and seat, with no space between them, and open wooden arms padded on top. It has no connection with the East Anglian artist Thomas Gainsborough, and was one of several types described by Chippendale as a 'French Chair'.

Gaming Table: an alternative term for a card table. In the early 19th century gaming tables of composite design achieved great popularity. They had reversible slides in the top for chess or draughts and interior provision for backgammon, etc. This type is generally known as a Games Table to distinguish it from a table devoted to one purpose only.

Gate-Leg Table: a circular, oval or rectangular table, usually made of oak, with two hinged flaps which, when raised, are supported on two or more pin-hinged legs which swing out like gates. Beginning as side-tables in the early 17th century, these tables were made

77

in large numbers after 1660 when a dining-room first became fashionable as a separate entity. They superseded the large fixed oak tables which had been universally used in the first half of the 17th century. Some gate-leg tables were of considerable size; most were fairly small and diners sometimes sat at several such tables in the same room. Rare examples fold completely flat, but the majority have a fixed central portion.

Gate-Leg Table

Georgian: an adjective which can be applied to any furniture, etc., made between the accession of George I in 1714 and the death of George IV in 1830, and is therefore too imprecise to denote the many succeeding styles of this long period when all the sovereigns happened to have the name of George. The Queen Anne style persisted into the reign of George I (1714–1727), overlapping the Palladian revival or William Kent style which was current until the middle of the century. It was succeeded, in the reign of George II (1727–1760), by the rococo or Chippendale style from about 1740, this being in turn superseded by the neo-classical or Adam style in the reign of George III (1760–1820), followed by the Hepplewhite and Sheraton renderings of the same mode in the last quarter of the 18th century and the Regency style from about 1800 to 1830. All these could be described as 'Georgian'.

Gesso: carbonate of lime mixed with parchment size (glue) used for surface ornament on furniture, picture-frames, etc., and usually gilded. It was first prevalent in medieval Italy where it was widely used on *cassoni* or chests, and because of its glistening whiteness, Titian used it to prime his canvases. It was extensively employed in England in the reign of Charles II and reached its peak during the Palladian revival in the time of William Kent when it was often used to decorate large coffers of sarcophagus form, some of them being extremely clumsy.

Gibbons, Grinling (1648–1720): English designer, sculptor and carver, born in Rotterdam of English parents. He was discovered at Deptford in 1671 by John Evelyn who introduced him to Sir Christopher Wren, and was thereafter responsible for splendid woodcarving in St. Paul's Cathedral, Windsor, Hampton Court, Oxford and Cambridge colleges, churches, mansions such as Petworth and Burleigh and sculpture in stone at Blenheim Palace. He was famous for his naturalistic rendering of foliage, flowers, birds, fruit, etc. Much of the work attributed to him was by contemporaries who profited by his example.

Gilding: gold has been applied to furniture since before the 2nd millenium B.C., notably in ancient Egypt, but received its chief impetus in Europe from medieval Italy, where the two main techniques were described by Cennini in the early 15th century. These consisted of water-gilding and oil-gilding, the first being the more brilli-

ant and the second the more durable. Both methods were being used in England in the late 17th century, and have been used ever since. The ground for water-gilding was gesso applied in several thin coats, the last of which was carefully smoothed and polished. It was then treated with a mordant to ensure the adhesion of the gold leaf which, against the hard, homogeneous underlying surface of gesso could be brightly burnished. The mordant employed in connection with oil-gilding consisted substantially of linseed oil which had been left in the sun until it thickened, and gold leaf applied to this sticky surface could not be burnished, though it had the advantage that it was impervious to damp and less likely to come off.

Gillow of Lancaster: celebrated cabinet-makers in the late 18th and early 19th centuries. Although Robert Gillow was established as a joiner in Lancaster in 1695, the firm does not seem to have gone in for cabinet-making until after 1731. The founder's sons, Richard, Thomas and Robert entered the business in about 1757, and in about 1770 the firm acquired premises in Oxford Street, London, though the stock continued for many years to be made in Lancaster. In 1800 Richard Gillow invented the telescopic dining-table. The family ceased to be connected with the business before 1820, though the name was retained doubtless for reasons of goodwill. The firm is best known for medium-quality furniture in the Adam and Regency styles at a time when the general standard was very high, and sold a great quantity in London and overseas. Many of the firm's productions, even in the 18th century, were stamped with its name: by no means a common practice in England at the time. Gillow's were probably the first cabinet-makers to make the small desk called a Davenport (*q.v.*).

Girandole: a term applied in the late 17th century to a wall sconce of any kind, but now generally implying a wall light from the rococo period to the Regency, often with a reflecting mirror, usually with a frame of carved and gilt wood and sconces for one or more candles. The arms of the sconces are often of gesso supported on an armature of iron wire.

Girandole (Rococo) c.1755

Glastonbury Chair: a popular name for a chair with lateral X-supports, panelled back and arms in the form of wings, probably introduced into England from Italy in the first half of the 16th century. An example at Wells, Somerset, reputedly belonged to the last Abbot of Glastonbury, hence the name. Genuine examples, mostly of the early 17th century, still survive in the chancels of many old churches, but there are numerous modern reproductions also.

Goodison, Benjamin: a highly-skilled London cabinet-maker who supplied many

Glastonbury Chair

items to the Royal household throughout the reign of George II and at the beginning of the reign of his successor. He probably died in 1766. One of his specialities was monumental looking-glasses in carved and gilt frames, but he made all kinds of other furniture as well, often sumptuously carved with acanthus leaves and large scallop-shell motifs.

Gothic Style: apart from denoting the architectural spirit which was dominant in applied art from the early 13th century to the early 16th century, this term is generally applied to various revival movements oc-

curring in the Georgian period. It was of little significance before the time of Chippendale (*q.v.*) when its first important manifestations appeared. Gothic details were then freely adapted and used in association with Chinese or rococo with pleasing results but without any straining after doctrinaire accuracy. The style was used again to a small extent during the Regency but was mostly confined to the glazing bars of cabinets and the windows of houses. See Chairs.

Grandfather Clock: see Long-Case Clock.

Greek Fret: See Key Pattern.

Grendey, Giles (1693-1780): a distinguished cabinet-maker of Clerkenwell, London, who flourished in the first half of the 18th century. His craftsmanship was excellent and his style unpretentious, though he developed an export business in japanned furniture of a decorative kind. Items which have been convincingly attributed to him show that he was particularly attached to fielded serpentine panels and serpentine frames in his cabinets.

Guéridon: a name now generally applied to any small table capable of holding a lamp, candlestick or candelabrum, especially if its design is under French influence. The name derives from that of a 17th-century Moorish slave, and early examples were sometimes in the form of a blackamoor supporting a platform upon which the light was placed.

Guilloche: running ornament of classical origin comprising interlaced strapwork in opposing curves producing series of almost circular compartments usually filled with conventional flower-heads of various kinds. It was first used on oak furniture of the 16th century but its incidence was higher after 1600.

Guilloche

It was occasionally employed in the 18th century, chiefly in the Adam period, being carved, painted or inlaid.

Gumley, John: first mentioned as a furniture-merchant in 1694, Gumley was a famous manufacturer of looking-glasses in the reigns of Queen Anne (1702–1714) and George I (1714–1727) and official purveyor to the latter. His glasshouse was established at Lambeth in 1705 and Richard Steele, in the *Spectator,* favourably compared his efficiency with that of the Duke of Buckingham. He later opened premises in the Strand and Norfolk Street and had accumulated a large fortune by his death in about 1728. His daughter married the Earl of Bath. A mirror, bearing Gumley's signature, is in the public dining-room at Hampton Court Palace.

H

H-Hinge: a surface hinge which was probably introduced in the 16th century but which continued in use throughout the 17th century and persisted after 1700. It consisted of two vertical plates, one each side of the central barrel, having something of the appearance of a letter H.

Haig, Thomas: see Chippendale.

Hall Cupboard: see Press Cupboard.

Harewood: an early 19th-century term for what had previously been called 'Air-wood': probably a corruption of the German *Ehrenholz*—maple. It consisted of maple or sycamore stained green with metallic oxides, and was extensively used for veneers in the late 18th century. It tends to turn grey with age.

Headboard: the vertical board at the head of a bed which prevents the pillows from slipping off.

Hepplewhite, George: cabinet-maker and designer who learnt his trade as an apprentice to Gillow of Lancaster (*q.v.*). He came to London at an unknown date and opened a shop in Cripplegate, where he died in 1786, having accumulated the material for his book of designs, *The Cabinet-maker and Upholsterer's Guide*, which was published by his widow in 1788. Two further editions appeared in 1789 and 1794, the latter containing many designs for square-backed chairs which superseded the shield-back in popularity in the last decade of the 18th century. As emendations of a technical kind were presumably beyond the powers of Hepplewhite's widow, it is probable that she received some assistance from Thomas Shearer (*q.v.*), who must have known her deceased husband and who was a designer in his own right. The author of the *Guide* claimed, in an excessively modest preface, only to have 'followed the latest or most prevailing fashion', thus avoiding any claim to originality, but although the designs were obviously eclectic, and reflected contemporary taste, the fact that surviving pieces of furniture are very seldom exactly like any of those illustrated indicates that Hepplewhite did not merely copy the work of others. The same fact suggests that the *Guide* was not so much a formative influence as a summary of contemporary trends, modified to some extent by the taste of the author, but his name has become a generic term for a simple, robust and elegant rendering of the neo-classical style of which Robert Adam was the chief protagonist. Oval- and shield-backed chairs, for example, are generally called 'Hepplewhite', though both shapes antedated the publication of the *Guide* by many years. Hepplewhite never had a considerable cabinet-making business or a fashionable clientéle, but the majority of the designs in his book are excellent. See Chairs and Sideboards.

Holland, Henry (1746–1806): architect and furniture-designer who achieved deserved fame for his modifications at Carlton

House in the late 18th century for George, Prince of Wales, and his work for Samuel Whitbread at Southill, for which he designed the interior and furniture in a version of the contemporary French *Directoire* style. The Adam style was still prevalent at the time, but it seems likely that Holland's work at Carlton House, which contained design ingredients which were to be further manifested in the taste of the early 19th century, may have precipitated a reaction against it. Had he lived longer his influence might have prevented or delayed the decadence which increasingly showed itself during the Regency.

Honeysuckle Ornament: see Anthemion.

Hoof-Foot: a kind of terminal, shaped like a hoof, occurring chiefly on early examples of the walnut cabriole leg for twenty years or so from about 1698; it was probably introduced to English chair-makers by Daniel Marot (*q.v.*).

Hope, Thomas (1769–1831): wealthy amateur and collector of classical sculpture and ceramics, who travelled extensively and studied ancient architecture in the erstwhile classical countries, Anatolia and Egypt. In 1807 he produced *Household Furniture and Decoration*, in which designs executed in his Surrey home, Deepdene, were illustrated. The furnishings of his London house, off Cavendish Square, prompted George Dance, the architect, to say 'it excited no feelings of comfort', while the designs in his book were received with varying degrees of approbrium by the critics, who possibly considered that a man without official professional status was not entitled to design anything. Some of his designs, however, although somewhat severe, had a certain quality of restrained purity which rendered them acceptable, for there is no doubt that, despite the strictures of the critics, his conceptions were widely copied. These included a 'monopodium', or circular table on a central support of splayed, concave triangular section, an example of which is preserved in the Victoria and Albert Museum, London, the feet, of massive lion-paw form, appearing often on other types of furniture.

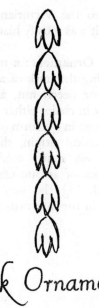

Husk Ornament

Horse Glass: see Cheval Glass.

Horsehair: mixed with wool, hair from the tails and manes of horses was widely used for stuffing upholstered furniture such as farthingale chairs in the early 17th century, and continued to be used thereafter for the same purpose. In the last quarter of the 18th century it often formed the weft-threads of a highly durable fabric for covering the seats of chairs, the warps being generally of linen. This fabric was sometimes striped in accordance with the prevailing taste, but continued

85

far into the Victorian period when it was mostly black.

Husk Ornament: a motif resembling the husk of a wheatgrain or beech nut, arranged usually in chains either straight or curved in the form of swags. Of classical origin, the ornament was much used in all branches of artistic craftsmanship during the neo-classical phase in the late 18th century.

Hutch: deriving originally from the French word *huche*, a kneading trough, this term has been used in England to denote many different things including an ordinary chest and a dole cupboard. It is now generally applied to a kind of large chest with canted or gabled top, often with perforated sides, to contain bread, most surviving specimens being of 17th-century date.

I

Ince and Mayhew: William Ince and John Mayhew were partners, from about 1759, in a cabinet-making and upholstery firm called Mayhew and Ince. Between 1759 and 1763 they brought out a book of some 300 furniture designs, based largely on Chippendale's *Director*, entitled the *Universal System of Household Furniture*. In this book were included designs for tripod tables, of which Chippendale had made no mention. Present-day references normally place Ince's name first as he was evidently the dominant and more active partner. Like Chippendale himself, whose designs they plagiarised with clumsy modification, Ince and Mayhew were not afflicted with excessive modesty: of a State Bed which they illustrated they said it 'may be esteemed among the best in England'.

Inlay: the decoration of furniture by cutting shaped recesses in the surface of the wood and insetting pieces of wood, ivory, metal, etc., of the same form but contrasting in tone or colour. It was a popular technique in the late 16th and early 17th centuries in England and should be distinguished from marquetry (*q.v.*).

J

Jacobean: an adjective deriving from the Latin *Jacobus*—James, applicable to furniture, etc., of the reign of James I (1603–1625) but often used to describe objects of the same essential character which were made up to about the middle of the 17th century. The Elizabethan style (*q.v.*) continued into the early part of the reign of James I, with a growing modification of previous excesses which is easier to recognise than describe. Carved ornament remained rich, but took on a tidier and less cluttered aspect. Bulbous protuberances disappeared from the legs of tables and the posts of beds and although the slimmer varieties of turned members retained the earlier forms, surfaces became more bland and reposeful. The same style lasted throughout the reign of Charles I (1625–1649), so it is not unreasonable to refer to objects of the first half of the 17th century as being in the Jacobean style, providing it is realised that this style was not confined to the reign of James I. See Chests and Credence.

Japanning: the process of decorating furniture with designs of an Oriental character in imitation of lacquer by means of various gums or resins, inspired by importations from the East chiefly by the East India Company in the early 17th century, though the traffic had already begun before 1600. Japanning attained great popularity after 1660 but had declined by the middle of the 18th century. It was revived early in the neo-classical period especially in connection with commodes (*q.v.*), the panels being either painted in England, made in China to fit English cabinet-frames, or cut from imported Oriental screens. The origins of the last-named are often evident from the fact that the scenes depicted are limited in an unreasonable manner, figures being sometimes headless or with feet amputated.

Jensen, Gerreit (active 1680-1715): cabinet-maker and supplier of mirrors to the Royal household from the reign of Charles II to the end of the reign of Queen Anne. He was one of the few craftsmen in England to inlay furniture with metal in the manner of André-Charles Boulle. He was almost certainly of Netherlandish origin, but in contemporary records his name was often anglicised to Gerrard or Garrett Johnson.

Johnson, Thomas: carver and furniture-designer who published two books of designs: *Twelve Girandoles* (1755) and *One Hundred and Fifty New Designs* (1756–1758, 2nd edition 1761). All these were in the rococo style with the frequent inclusion of human and animal forms. Many of his designs were weak and impracticable, but he was an excellent draughtsman and an accomplished craftsman.

Joined Stool: a stool—also known as a Joynt Stool—of pegged construction, having four turned legs united by stretchers, made by joiners from the middle of the 16th century and taking the place of the slab-ended or plank stools previously made by carpenters. The legs were fluted or occasionally gadrooned until the early 17th century when the turnings were normally left plain. The wooden top was usually covered by a cushion. Joined stools are often miscalled 'coffin stools'. They were the normal seating furniture used about the dining-table, and after a meal were commonly stowed away beneath it.

Joined Stool

Jousting Chest: a modern term for a type of chest of the 14th century carved in relief on the front panel with figures

89

of mounted knights jousting with lances. It is also known less correctly as a Tilting Chest —an inaccurate term, as tilting was a course in which the contestants were separated by a barrier or tilt, and this is never shown on the chests in question.

K

Kauffmann, Angelica (1741–1807): an accomplished painter, Angelica Kauffmann was born in Switzerland and came to London about 1766. She was highly esteemed and was elected to the Royal Academy as one of the original members in 1768. She married another artist, Antonio Zucchi, in 1781, after being ostensibly married to a plausible scoundrel who already had a wife. She was given many commissions by the Adam brothers for the decoration of walls and ceilings and designed ornament for painted furniture, almost certainly executing some of it herself. Her designs were widely used by other artists.

Kent, William (1686–1748): architect and designer, went to Italy in 1710 to study painting, for which, however, he never had any great aptitude. While there, he met the future Earl of Leicester and the 3rd Earl of Burlington, an accomplished architect, who became his friend and patron. He returned to London in 1719, Burlington's patronage ensuring for him a dominant position as an arbiter of taste in architecture and interior design. Kent's style was ponderous and there was some contemporary criticism of his 'heavy hand', but as his manner accorded with prevailing taste he was much in demand. His furniture was usually decorated with large-scale ornament of a rich and sumptuous character, involving the use of acanthus foliage, classical masks and terminal figures executed with great realism. His designs for case-furniture were often heavily architectural in style, three-door cabinets, for example, looking like the fronts of renaissance buildings, surmounted by broken triangular pediments with deep returns. His taste in this respect was almost certainly conditioned by his admiration for the 16th-century Italian architect, Andrea Palladio, whose work he had seen in Italy, and for this reason he is regarded as a moving spirit, with Burlington, in the contemporary 'Palladian revival'. He must receive credit for being the first British architect to strive for consistency of feeling in his interiors, so that all the details formed part of a harmonious whole.

Kettle-Stand: introduced in the late 17th century for the silver tea-kettle and its spirit lamp, these stands were chiefly in the form of low tripod tables, a few being made of solid silver. The tops were circular, square or

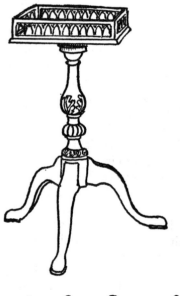

Kettle-Stand

triangular, often with a gallery round the edge. Another type, introduced in the rococo period, had four legs and a box-top usually lined with metal, and a slide for the teapot below. All these special stands for kettles went out of fashion in about 1800, ordinary occasional tables being used thereafter. Kettle-stands were lower than contemporary tripod tables so that the kettle, mounted on its lamp-stand, would be at a convenient height. The type has been reproduced by the thousand for many years, and they are usually described as 'wine-tables': a purpose for which they were never intended in the 18th century.

Key Pattern

Key Pattern: known otherwise as Greek Fret, and consisting of a repetitive border design in several variations containing straight lines changing direction at right-angles. Deriving from architectural ornament of ancient Greece, it was prevalent in the time of William

Kent and again in the Adam period and the early 19th century. It was either carved in low relief, painted or inlaid.

Kingwood: a Brazilian wood first imported into England in the second half of the 17th century when it was known as Princewood or Prince's Wood. The latter remained its name until the early Victorian period. It was mostly employed in the form of veneer and, in the late 17th century, sometimes covered entire cabinets. It fell out of favour in about 1700, but in the second half of the 18th century began to be used extensively for cross-banding. It is normally light in tone with darker streaks, and sometimes looks like pale rosewood, of which it is a botanical relative.

Knee-Hole Tables: these tables are of various kinds, the earliest being introduced in the late 17th century and having legs and drawers each side of a central arch. Soon after 1700 another type appeared with a central recess, usually with a cupboard in it, and tiers of small drawers on each side resting on bracket feet or rudimentary legs of the same height. The knee-hole in this variant is very inadequate for the purpose as the recess is insufficiently deep. Both kinds could be used either for writing or as dressing-tables. When primarily devoted to the latter purpose they usually had a small toilet-mirror standing on the top. Later examples from the mid-18th century sometimes had lift-up tops disclosing dressing fitments. Library tables of the mahogany period usually had wide knee-holes and pedestals of drawers and/or cupboards, but are not classified as knee-hole tables.

Knife-Case c.1775

Knife-Case: a box container, with sloping top and shaped corners, in which knives and flatware were stored vertically in sockets, was in use before 1650, and essentially the same type continued throughout the 18th century. They were made of various woods, sometimes covered with shagreen or mounted in silver, while a few were of solid silver. During the Adam period an urn-shape was introduced with a cover which was raised and lowered on a central stem. This type was designed to stand on a pedestal at either end of a sideboard without drawers or, if other urns intended to contain water occupied the same position, on the top of the sideboard itself.

L

Laburnum: a hard, yellowish wood with brown markings which became naturalised in England at about the beginning of the 17th century and was used by cabinet-makers chiefly in the form of oyster veneer (*q.v.*).

Ladder-Back Chair: a type of chair with horizontal slats or cross-rails between the uprights, introduced into England in the late 17th century, probably from the Netherlands, where it was well established by 1600. The slats were first carved into scrolls, some early examples being made of walnut, but a simpler form, made usually of ash and with a rush seat, began to be made after 1700 in large numbers, continuing throughout the 18th century unaffected by the changing fashions which conditioned chairs of higher quality. From about 1760 a more sophisticated version in mahogany enjoyed some popularity, persisting into the Adam period sometimes with neo-classical motifs such as the anthemion in the centre of the slats.

Ladder-Back Chair c.1710

Langley, Batty and Thomas: architects and designers, the talented Langley brothers published, in 1740, the *City and Country Builder's and Workman's Treasury of Designs,* deriving largely from Continental originals but of a high general level of excellence. The publication was successful but its influence was short-lived, as the furniture which it illustrated was in a style which was soon to be superseded by the rococo (*q.v.*).

Library Steps: occurred sparsely in the late 17th century but did not come into general use until about 1750. Some were of fixed construction, often with handrails, others folded away into the tops of tables or were embodied in stools or in chairs, the backs of which hinged over to rest on the floor, thus exposing the steps.

Library Tables: library tables of pedestal-desk form were known in the reign of Charles II (1660–1685) but were of the utmost rarity until the second quarter of the 18th century. With the adoption of mahogany by cabinet-makers their manufacture steadily increased, and they were illustrated by Chippendale, Hepplewhite and Sheraton. In the last quarter of the 18th century they were sometimes oval—a form deriving from classical paterae—or kidney-shaped, and were sometimes made of satinwood like other furniture of the period. Although the two-pedestal type

continued into the Regency, a small, circular variety, now often known as a 'drum table', enjoyed some popularity. All these tables, which could be used for both reading and writing, normally stood in the centre of the library.

Linenfold Pattern: a modern term for a repetitive design carved on wall panelling or furniture of panelled construction such as chests, chairs, beds, etc., suggestive of folded linen. The folds are usually vertical, but are sometimes horizontal; popular in the late 15th and early 16th centuries. The design was introduced to England from the duchy of Burgundy in the late 15th century, but was more prevalent in the first quarter of the 16th century, after which its incidence waned.

Linnell, John (*c.* **1735–1796**): carver, cabinet-maker and designer who worked in the rococo and associated Chinese and Gothic styles, but also executed work for Robert Adam in the neo-classical manner. He was considered as being in the first rank of his profession and had a number of distinguished clients. His designs were never published, but some of them are preserved in the Victoria and Albert Museum, London.

Livery Cupboard: a name sometimes given to a food cupboard, usually pierced for ventilation, from the medieval period to the mid-17th century. The word derives from the French *livrer,* to deliver. In wealthy households livery cupboards were often present in bed-chambers so that guests could help themselves to food during the night if they felt hungry.

Lobby Chest: a small chest of drawers. Sheraton defined it as 'a kind of half chest of drawers, adapted for the use of a small study, lobby, etc.'.

Lock, Matthias: designer and carver, and probably the first exponent of an English version of the French *rocaille* (rococo) style. From 1740 he published books and designs in this novel idiom either alone or in collaboration with Henry Copland (*q.v.*), his last publication appearing in 1769. Lock and Copland were employed by Thomas Chippendale in the production of his *Director*, and were evi-dently responsible for many of the designs for which Chippendale took the credit.

Long-Case Clocks: weight-driven bracket-clocks, which existed in fairly large numbers by the third quarter of the 17th century, had the weights hanging down below the brackets where their action was liable to be impeded by accidental contact with extraneous objects. The introduction of the long-case clock arose partly from a desire to obviate this inconvenience by enclosing the whole within a wooden case resting on the floor, partly to house the pendulum, especially the longer variety perfected by Hooke in 1666.

The clocks themselves are of great technical interest and may be studied in specialised works; here, we are concerned, not with horology but with furniture, and long-case clocks will accordingly be considered in regard to their outward appearance inasmuch as the manufacture of the cases was an important branch of cabinet-making.

Early cases of the reign of Charles II were often no taller than an average man and many were made of oak. Superior examples were veneered with ebony and were surmounted by hoods with triangular or segmental pediments (*q.v.*) with the corners of the architraves resting on columns with gilt Corinthian capitals. The faces were square and the spandrels between the corners and the circular chapter-rings bearing the figures were commonly filled with decorative motifs such as boys and crowns (*q.v.*) or winged cherubs' heads in gilt brass; the latter were of renaissance origin and had occurred on silverware of the Elizabethan period.

By 1670 long-case clocks were usually from six to seven feet high. The columns on the hoods were often twist-turned like the legs and uprights of chairs, etc., and the cornices were generally horizontal, though swan-necked pediments were occasionally found from about 1685. Walnut veneers became more popular than the sombre ebony, and the various forms of marquetry occurring on other contemporary furniture continued on clock-cases into the reign of Queen Anne. At the same time it was often the practice to provide a small circular window in the door of the case so that the movement

of the weights and pendulum could be seen. This feature did not persist much beyond about 1725 in the metropolis but continued rather longer in the provinces.

In the last years of the 17th century the hood was sometimes crowned by a flattened dome of varying profile and usually of rectangular section, and thereafter the plain, horizontal cornice was seldom found. Chinoiserie ornament was sometimes used as an alternative to decorative veneers until after 1750.

A change in the shape of the clock face began to appear in the early 18th century, though it was not generally adopted at once. This took the form of a semicircular extension at the top which affected the shape of the wooden frame by necessitating the provision of a round arch which was often emphasised by projecting mouldings. This detail remained widely current for the rest of the 18th century. The tops of hoods began to be embellished with small urns or balls of gilt wood or brass, and this detail also, although not universal, was found on many examples throughout the century.

When mahogany superseded

walnut as the fashionable material for furniture in the first half of the 18th century it was used for the cases of clocks as well. Most surviving examples of good quality are either made of this wood or veneered with it. During the Chippendale period, a small amount of carving or blind fretting in the rococo, Chinese or Gothic styles sometimes occurred, though the doors of the cases were usually left plain, relying for their effect on the grain of the polished wood, and at the same time, pilasters were occasionally contrived at the angles between the fronts and sides.

During the neo-classical phase, in the time of Hepplewhite and Sheraton (*q.q.v.*), satinwood appeared on clock cases in the form of all-over or partial veneer, and attempts were made to break away from the traditional shape which had been current since the reign of Charles II. Movements were enclosed in small, circular cases standing on classical pedestals or flattened balusters containing the weights and pendulums. These clocks had an elegant and refined appearance, but were nevertheless greatly outnumbered by the more sturdy-looking traditional types which

continued to be made far into the 19th century.

Lopers: a word of Dutch origin used in the late 17th and early 18th centuries for the runners which, when pulled out, supported the falls of bureaux, etc.

Love-Seat: an upholstered settee for two persons.

Lozenge Ornament: a motif of diamond shape, usually carved with a gouge, often found on oak furniture from

Lyre-Back
(Adam)

the late 16th century until after 1660. It lingered on in the provinces and the American colonies long after it was abandoned in London.

Lunette: a half-moon shape; in connection with furniture indicating ornament in the form of semicircles usually arranged in rows. It was common on oak furniture especially in the early 17th century and occurred again in the late 18th century when it was often inlaid or painted on satinwood commodes.

Lyre-Back Chair: a chair of the late 18th-century neoclassical period with a splat deriving in shape from a classical lyre and having 'strings' of wood or metal. Robert Adam designed chairs of this type, and in none of them is there any straining after verisimilitude, the lyreform being used merely as a basic shape, but some of his followers used the design in a more literal manner which is less pleasing. Some of the latter had thin brass 'strings'.

M

Mahogany: although Sir Walter Raleigh is said to have shown Queen Elizabeth a sample of mahogany in the late 16th century and it was undoubtedly known in the reign of Charles II, it was not until after 1720 that it began to be imported in any quantity for the manufacture of furniture. The traffic was stimulated by the ban by the French government on the export of Grenoble walnut in that year. In 1721 an Act was passed by the British parliament exempting timber from British plantations in America from import duty, and although Virginia walnut naturally benefited as well, a result of the Act was that the eyes of timber importers were turned exclusively towards the Americas. It was thus inevitable that certain superior qualities that mahogany possessed, such as the largeness of planks and resistance to rot and the ravages of woodworm, should soon be noticed.

Its steadily increasing popularity is evident from the fact that the value of mahogany imported in 1722 was £276, but the annual value by the end of the 18th century was almost £80,000. Spanish merchants also shared in the trade. Mahogany from the Spanish settlements was transhipped at Jamaica, and entered England as wood from British plantations. In this connection it should be noted that mahogany trees have never grown in Spain; the term 'Spanish mahogany' simply means timber from the Spanish-American colonies. The traffic increased after 1733, when Sir Robert Walpole abolished the import duty on timber altogether. Initially, Jamaica, Puerto Rico and San Domingo were the principal sources of supply, but before the middle of the 18th century Cuban mahogany became highly esteemed for its richness of colour and the strongly-marked patterns in the grain of certain cuts.

Timber from Honduras was also used and was known as 'baywood', but it has an uninteresting grain and lacks density, the latter characteristic accounting for the lightness of weight displayed by certain chairs, etc., of the later 18th century. But although its surface-quality was considered inferior to that of other types, it was often used in the solid for the carcase-work of the best furniture, important parts such as fronts and door-panels being veneered with Cuban mahogany. Most old mahogany retains its red colour, which is consistent throughout its substance owing to the methods of seasoning employed, but San Domingo mahogany tends to turn black with age.

Manwaring, Robert: cabinet-maker and designer who was best known for his chairs. In 1765 he published *The Cabinet and Chair Makers' Real Friend and Companion*, a very unequal work indeed. He had an excessively high opinion of the designs in this short book, but some of the chairs had a good deal of merit and were actually made. Many were entirely typical of the period and naturally had a family resemblance to Chippendale's, but one distinctive design showed backs consisting of large inter-

laced circles or ovals. Some of these have survived and are occasionally to be seen in contemporary paintings. In 1766, Manwaring was joint author of a work entitled *The Chairmakers' Guide*, which included some of his earlier designs. Sheraton, in his *Drawing Book* (1791), dismissed *The Chairmakers' Guide* in contemptuous terms, but it is probable that his criticisms of Manwaring and others were largely conditioned by bitterness at his own undeserved ill-fortune.

Marot, Daniel: architect and designer of furniture, silverware, etc. Though enjoying some esteem in his native France, Marot was a Huguenot, and it appears that in 1684 he got wind of the impending persecution of his co-religionists by Louis XIV and left France for the Netherlands, before the revocation of the Edict of Nantes in 1685 endowed the persecution with ostensible legality. He soon became *persona grata* at the Hague in the court of the Stadholder who became King William III of England in 1689, and in 1694 followed him to London where he remained for four years before returning to Holland. While in England he exerted a significant influence on furniture design, and almost certainly introduced the cabriole leg, which was already well established in France, to English chair-makers.

Marquetry: the decoration of furniture by cutting veneers of contrasting tones or colours into patterns and, after fitting them together, gluing the resultant sheet on to a prepared carcase. The design was drawn on paper which was stuck on the surface of the uppermost of several sheets of different veneers fixed together one above the other, the number depending on the colours required. The lines of the pattern were then cut through all the layers with a fine saw. It thus followed, with mathematical certainty, that a shaped piece of veneer cut out of the top sheet would fit into the space created by the removal of the corresponding piece from the sheet below. When the pattern was assembled, a sheet of paper glued to the top held it together. The surface of the piece of furniture to be decorated was then made level and uniformly roughened with a tool to provide a 'tooth'. The

sheet of marquetry was glued on, and when adhesion was complete the paper was removed and the marquetry polished. The process, of which the above is a simplified account, was introduced soon after 1660, and remained popular until the early 18th century, continuing rather longer on clock-cases than on other furniture. It was revived in about 1765 and persisted into the early 19th century, being especially prevalent on commodes of the Adam period. See also Inlay.

Marsh, William: cabinet-maker and upholsterer, supplied much furniture for Carlton House and Brighton Pavilion before 1800, his work enjoying a high reputation. In about 1800 the firm became Marsh and Tatham and in 1807, Tatham and Bailey, adding another partner, Saunders, in 1811. The firm at this time were the chief upholsterers to the Prince of Wales, the future George IV.

Medallion: a compartment, chiefly circular or oval, containing a decorative device usually of a classical and animate nature. An early example on English furniture is the Romayne heads (*q.v.*) of the early 16th century, but the medallion was chiefly used during the Adam period, when it was carved, painted or inlaid and usually contained a head or figures, or, less frequently, flowers.

Military Chest: known otherwise as a Campaign Chest. Various items of military furniture were in use in the French army in the 18th century, and were probably used by British military travellers in the early 19th century, but there is almost no reliable information available concerning the chests of drawers commonly known as military chests. The National Army Museum has no evidence that they were ever officially issued or even officially approved, while the fact that a number were in teak suggests not only that these might have been made in the Orient, but also that they were just as likely to have been used on board ship as on land. Some were made of other timbers including mahogany and even camphorwood but nearly all were constructed in the same manner. They took apart horizontally across the centre, the

feet could be unscrewed, the corners were reinforced with brass, and the flat-fronted loop-handles were accommodated in brass-lined recesses to obviate awkward projections. The top drawer sometimes had a fall-front disclosing a secretaire (*q.v.*). Most surviving specimens date from the Victorian era and the vast majority have no known military associations.

Mirror-Stand: a tall, slender pole on tripod base with an adjustable mirror which could be fixed in any position desired by means of a screw; late 18th century.

Monopodium: a name given by Thomas Hope (*q.v.*) in the early 19th century to a circular table having a central support of triangular section with concave sides, the base angles terminating in elaborate paw feet (*q.v.*).

Moore, James (*c.* 1670–1726): cabinet-maker and partner to John Gumley (*q.v.*). He assisted in the furnishing of Blenheim Palace and specialised in the making of furniture, including looking-glass frames, decorated with gilt gesso on which he sometimes incised his name.

Mortice and Tenon: a type of furniture joint, introduced about the middle of the 16th century, involving the use of an oblong or square hole (mortice) into which a tongue (tenon) fits.

Mortuary Chair: a jargon term for a type of chair or backstool made in Yorkshire and Derbyshire in the mid-17th century. The backs of these chairs had two arched crossrails often carved in relief with a face with a pointed beard, the features being usually only perfunctorily indicated by incisions, and this detail is sometimes erroneously supposed to represent King Charles I who, in any event, was probably still alive when the type first appeared. In fact, carved faces of the kind in question had frequently occurred on grotesque figures forming part of the decoration of chests, headboards of beds, etc., in the Elizabethan period. See Derbyshire Chair.

Mule Chest: a chest originating in the 16th century, but rare until the middle of the 17th century, having one or two drawers in the base of the front.

Muntin: a vertical member of the framework of a piece of furniture other than those at both ends (see Stiles). On panelled chests of the 16th and 17th centuries, the muntins were connected to the upper and lower horizontal portions of the framework between the panels. On commodes of the late 18th century they often took the form of pilasters (*q.v.*) and were sometimes prolonged downwards to form additional legs.

Mushroom Turning: a turned protuberance somewhat like the cap of a mushroom occurring on the legs of furniture between 1690 and shortly after 1700. It could be of square or circular section.

Nest of Drawers: a miniature chest of drawers for the storage of small objects occurring in the 18th and 19th centuries. They are often regarded as apprentices' essays or travellers' samples, though there is little evidence to support either notion.

Night-Table: a kind of bedside cabinet, usually of admirable workmanship, which appeared in the second quarter of the 18th century and was almost invariably made of mahogany. The top was surrounded by a complete or partial gallery and a cupboard below was provided for a chamber-pot. This was enclosed in various ways: by one or two doors, depending on the width, by a single piece of wood with a spring-loaded knob handle which, on being pulled to release it from a catch, caused the front to drop downwards, or, from about 1765, by a tambour (*q.v.*) working horizontally. Some examples embodied a close-stool in the lower part which could

Night-Table

be pulled out when required. See Commode.

Nonsuch (Nonesuch) Ornament: an English term for inlaid decoration of furniture in the form of extravagant architecture with pinnacles and cupolas, occurring on such items as chest-fronts and portable desks from about 1540. The name refers to Henry

VIII's palace of Nonsuch at Cheam in Surrey, which was based on designs by Toto del Nunziata. Ornament of this kind probably originated in Italy, but quite possibly reached England from Germany without any connection with the palace from which its name is derived. Some pieces of furniture bearing Nonsuch ornament and long regarded as English may well have been imported. The style remained moderately popular for about fifty years.

Nulling: see Gadrooning.

O

Oak: a hard, native wood generally used for furniture from the middle ages to the middle of the 17th century when walnut became fashionable, but continuing to be employed thereafter up to the 19th century, especially in provincial areas, as an alternative to more expensive timbers in vogue at various periods but in similar styles. The once extensive English oak forests had become so reduced by the demands of house-building, ship-construction, furniture-making and industry by the early 16th century that Henry VIII gave his assent to an Act aimed at their conservation. It appears that this statute was widely evaded, for James I, in 1615, found it necessary to publish a decree forbidding the use of all kinds of wood as an industrial fuel. Some re-afforestation had been undertaken under Elizabeth but this could have no effect for at least a hundred years, so a softer species of oak was extensively imported from Germany and Scandinavia, usually under the name of 'wainscot', up to the middle of the 17th century. By the latter part of the century the decline of timbered buildings and the use of coal by the iron-workers and glass-makers had evidently relieved the situation, and English oak began to be openly used again for carcase-work and drawer-linings on walnut and, later, mahogany furniture, though some was imported as well. Oak has a somewhat open grain and takes a long time to develop a satisfying patine, but once it has done so it has a durable surface-quality which no maker of reproductions can convincingly simulate.

Ogee: a flattened S-curve, called by the artist William Hogarth 'the line of beauty'.

Olive: a yellowish wood with dark markings sometimes used for veneering entire surfaces of card-tables, bureaux, etc., in the Georgian period, but employed in a more distinguished manner for oystering (*q.v.*) in the late 17th and early 18th centuries.

Ormolu: an English form of the French *or moulu*—ground gold—denoting a technique used in France from the renaissance period for applying gold to other metals as an alternative to normal fire-gilding. The term has been used in England since the mid-18th century to indicate gilt brass and bronze, especially in connection with mounts for furniture. These were used by Chippendale on 'commode tables' and other objects under French influence, but became even more prevalent during the Adam period, when Matthew Boulton of Birmingham, otherwise distinguished for the manufacture of domestic plate, was the most celebrated maker, his work being equal to the best produced in France.

Ottoman: known also as a Turkey Sofa and consisting of a low upholstered seat providing accommodation for several persons, named in reference to the Ottoman Empire and described by Sheraton (*q.v.*) in the *Drawing Book* as being in 'imitation of the Turkish mode of sitting'. George Smith (*q.v.*) defined it in his *Household Furniture* of 1808 as a long couch. Ottomans were made throughout the 19th century and were sometimes in the form of an upholstered chest with hinged lid.

Overstuffed Seat: the seat of a chair, settee, etc., in which the upholstery fabric covers the seat rails and is secured by tacks underneath. Such pieces of furniture were often described in the 18th century as being 'stuffed over the rails'.

Ovolo Moulding: a classical architectural moulding of quadrant-section, either plain of surface or with egg-and-dart ornament, sometimes used for the cornices of case-furniture in the 16th and 17th centuries and on the frames of looking-glasses from about 1660.

Oyster-Pieces, Oyster Veneer, Oystering: veneers made by cutting thin sections through the branches of strongly-marked woods such as walnut, olive, laburnum and yew. When glued side by side on to the carcase of a cabinet the annual rings on the veneers gave something of the appearance of oysters. The sections were cut square round the edges to enable them to be assembled without difficulty, and are often so skilfully cut and applied that the joints between them are scarcely discernible. Oystering was popular in the late 17th and early 18th centuries, and was usually allied with walnut. Oyster-pieces of yew may sometimes be distinguished by fine cracks along the medullary rays.

P

Pad Foot: a variant of the club foot (*q.v.*) usually on cabriole legs, with a short cylinder or pad of wood beneath; popular from the early 18th century.

Padouk: a hard, dense timber from Burma and the Andaman Islands brown or red in colour, often with darker lines and undulations in the grain, used sparsely in the first half of the 18th century and very occasionally later for chairs. A false impression has been created by the fact that such pieces of furniture were sometimes made locally to English designs in the countries where the timber was found, and were subsequently imported into England.

Palladian: a style based on that of the 16th-century Italian architect Andrea Palladio who designed a number of distinguished renaissance villas in the north of Italy; used by Inigo Jones in the early 17th century and revived by the Earl of Burlington and William Kent in the first half of the 18th century, when it was applied to architecture, decoration and furniture of a heavily architectural character. English looking-glasses of the period were particularly successful, their frames apparently deriving from Palladian window-frames.

Papier-Mâché: a composition of Persian origin whose constituents varied after its introduction into England in the late 17th century but which always contained paper. It may have lain in oblivion for a while, as a manufacturer named Peter Babel of London, who advertised various sorts of papier-mâché items of furniture in 1763, described it as an 'invention of modern date'. Henry Clay of Birmingham patented an improved process of manufacture in 1772 which resulted in the production of small articles of furniture not mentioned by Babel, such as trays, though cabinets were made as well, many having the appearance of Oriental lacquer. Clay's process consisted of sticking layers of paper together, so that it was not really *mâché*, but it achieved a considerable measure of success, items of furniture made of his 'paper-ware' being supplied to aristocratic clients. Papier-mâché was especially popular in the 19th century. Jennens and Beteridge started a factory in Birmingham which became famous for its tea-trays, and were probably the first undertaking to introduce mother-of-pearl into the surface of the composition. In the event, this refinement marked the beginning of a decadence, for, used on an increasingly lavish scale, it made objects pretty but tended to destroy their dignity.

Parquetry: an English term deriving from the French *parqueterie*—inlay—having the special sense of inlay either directly into the wood or by means of veneer, in geometrical patterns of any kind. The technique was chiefly current at the same time as marquetry (*q.v.*), namely, in the late 17th and early 18th centuries and again in the late 18th century.

Patera (plural, Paterae): a flat

ornamental motif of classical architectural origin, either circular or oval. The word is a Latin noun of the first declension denoting a shallow cup, often with symmetrical ornament inside, used for pouring libations in religious ceremonies. During the classical revival in the second half of the 18th century, paterae were frequently employed as decoration on buildings, furniture, etc. On chairs, for example, they often occurred in the backs

Paterae

and sometimes formed a major part of the splat; a favourite situation was at the tops of the front legs, level with the seat rails. If the chair was of mahogany the paterae were mostly carved in slight relief; if satinwood, they were usually painted or inlaid. They also conditioned the shape of most of the drawer handles of the period. The term has been extended to include similar ornament of rectangular form occupying a space of the same shape; these are known as square paterae. All types continued to some extent into the early 19th century. See also Medallion.

Paw Foot: the foot of a cabriole leg in the form of a lion's paw, prevalent in the second quarter of the 18th century on furniture of all kinds, the earlier being usually

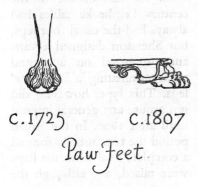

c.1725   c.1807

Paw Feet

carved to indicate fur. On the legs of chairs the paw foot often appears disproportionately large, but is a pleasing feature of cabinets as its ponderous aspect is congruous with the large mass above. A longer variant, with a scrolled rearward extension, appeared in the early 19th century on the bases of tables, wine-coolers, etc., the type being illustrated by Thomas Hope (*q.v.*).

Pear: the wood of the pear tree is heavy and with a homogeneous grain, and it was used in all periods for country-made furniture. In the 16th and 17th centuries it was sometimes stained black and polished to simulate ebony, being used for inlay, as veneer and, in the solid, for the frames of pictures and looking-glasses, though its use was never widespread for sophisticated cabinet-work.

Péché-Mortel: a French term for a couch, probably absorbed into English in the second quarter of the 18th century. Thomas Chippendale illustrated two examples with rococo ornament and having a somewhat French appearance, and it is possible that English usage confined the term to couches inspired by French originals.

Pedestal Table: another name for a tripod table or claw table supported, above the legs, on a central pillar or pedestal.

Pediment: the original pediment of ancient Greece took the form of a triangular surmount above the entablature at

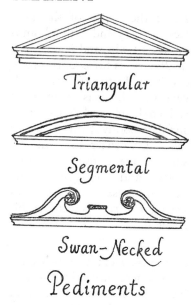

Triangular

Segmental

Swan-Necked

Pediments

Pembroke Table: a name which first appeared in the mid-18th century denoting a small table with two hinged flaps which were supported, when raised, on fly-brackets which could be swung out from the side of the framework. They achieved great popularity in the last quarter of the 18th century when examples were illustrated by Hepplewhite and Sheraton. Until the last decade of the century Pembroke tables had always had the usual four legs, but Sheraton designed a variant supported on a central pillar terminating in four 'claw' legs. This type, however, did not arouse any general interest until after 1800. In the Adam period the tops usually formed a complete oval when the flaps were raised, and although the

the end of a building, for example, the Parthenon at Athens. Several types of pediment were in use in the architecture of the renaissance period apart from the triangular, such as the segmental, shaped like a segment of a circle, the broken pediment, with the central section absent, and the swan-necked pediment in the form of two opposed wave-crests. All were used to a very slight extent on English furniture of the late 17th century but were extremely popular from the early 18th century on furniture conceived under architectural influence.

Pembroke Table c.1780

114

majority were in plain mahogany, sometimes cross-banded round the edge, some were made of satinwood painted or inlaid with typical neo-classical ornament such as swags, paterae, medallions, etc., or conceived as complete oval paterae and decorated accordingly. A rectangular shape was also used for tops, or a hybrid between it and an oval consisting of a rectangle with rounded corners. Treatment became more massive during the Regency with a corresponding loss of elegance.

Pergolesi, Michele Angelo: immigrant Italian artist and designer and author of *Original Designs* which was issued in fourteen parts between 1777 and 1801 when Pergolesi died. It contained designs for the decoration of walls, ceilings and furniture, some of the last being carried out. It is possible that he may have worked for the Adam brothers like many of his compatriots.

Pier Glass: a kind of tall looking-glass, popular throughout the 18th century, designed to be attached to the narrow piece of wall between windows.

Pier Table: a side-table, flat along the back, designed to stand against the piece of wall between windows which constituted a pier in the architectural sense, usually beneath a pier glass. Pier tables varied in height as it was considered desirable that their tops should be level with the dado round the walls. In the late 18th century the majority had tops in the shape of half ovals or semicircles. Examples made of satinwood were often decorated in a manner which suggests that they were thought of as halved paterae.

Pilaster: a partial column, not in the round but with the appearance of having been divided vertically, applied to a flat surface in architecture or on furniture. Pilasters, which could be of any section, occurred from the 16th century but were especially prevalent in the 18th century. During the Palladian (*q.v.*) revival they were often of precise architectural type like many other contemporary details, and were applied to cabinets so that they were complementary to the pediments above. Their proportions were refined during the second half of the century and they frequently occurred on neo-classical commodes either flat or as colonnettes (*q.v.*).

Pin-Hinge: generally confined to chests in the 13th century and consisting of a stout pin running through the flange at either end of the lid into the rear stiles. The head of the pin was usually covered with a small metal plate, shaped like a kite or Norman shield, to prevent withdrawal.

Pine: the wood of pine and spruce trees was hardly ever used for furniture in England until after 1660 owing to the ready availability of oak, but with the introduction of the practice of veneering it began to be employed for carcasework. It was also much in demand for carved objects destined to be gilded and for wall-panelling in the second half of the 18th century, when it was invariably painted.

Plane: the wood of the plane tree was sometimes used in the 18th century for painted furniture as an alternative to beech.

Plateau: a long, low platform with rounded ends, supported usually on many small feet like

those of a salver, placed down the centre of a dining-table in the late 18th and early 19th centuries. Plateaux were frequently made in sections, somewhat like the leaves of a table, so that they could be lengthened or shortened at will. They were of metal, wood or papier-mâché and were commonly decorated with ornament of the prevailing type. Despite their evident popularity, there appear to be few survivals.

Plate Pail: a circular or polygonal mahogany pail with a brass swing-handle and an opening down one side, designed for carrying plates between the kitchen and dining-room and occurring from the mid-18th century. Some were of robust construction with brass hoops like those of a common type of wine-cooler, others had the sides pierced with Gothic or 'Chinese' fret.

Pole-Screen: see Fire-Screen.

Poplar: a light-coloured wood with a close grain used to some extent in the 16th and 17th centuries for inlay or marquetry but seldom applied to any other purpose owing to its tendency to shrink.

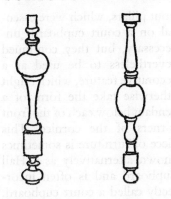

Portuguese Swell

Portuguese Swell: a type of turning occurring on the legs of furniture for a little over a decade from about 1690, and consisting either of an inverted baluster with a boldly emphasised protuberance or a cylindrical shaft with a ball knop.

Press: an alternative name for a storage cupboard, often occurring in combination with other terms, for example, clothes-press (*q.v.*), etc.

Press Bed: a bed which could be folded away into a cupboard or wardrobe. Press beds were current chiefly from the late 17th century to the late 18th century, when they began to be regarded in fashionable circles as anachronistic, though they continued to be used by servants far into the 19th century. Contemporary records show that great ingenuity often went into their construction, the cupboard doors, hinged at the top, being raised up and supported on separate posts to form a tester, and the bed and bedstead emerging from the interior of the press with hinged legs attached to the base of the frame to support the bed in a horizontal position. A letter from Horace Walpole in 1755 mentioned that the house of the Duke of Newcastle in Chelsea contained a press bed for a servant in the duke's

Press Cupboard

bed-chamber, as he was afraid to sleep alone.

Press Cupboard: a hybrid, in the late 16th and 17th centuries, between a fully enclosed press and a court cupboard (*q.v.*), having usually two stages, the upper recessed with first one and later two doors beneath a projecting cornice, and the lower with two larger doors. The enclosed construction ensured adequate support for the top and rendered the front pillars, which were essential on a court cupboard, unnecessary, but they continued nevertheless to be used as a decorative feature, which might otherwise take the form of a pendant below each of the front corners of the cornice. This piece of furniture is sometimes known alternatively as a Hall Cupboard and is often incorrectly called a court cupboard.

Prince's Wood or Princewood: see Kingwood.

Q

Quadrant Beading: a beading having a quarter-circle section, which began to be applied to the inside of drawers between the sides and the base in furniture of the best quality from about 1790. It became more common after 1800, when its advantages were realised.

Quartetto Tables: nests of four small tables with slender turned legs, made in slightly diminishing sizes so that the smaller fitted beneath the larger. They first appeared in the early 19th century and were mostly in either mahogany or rosewood.

R

Reading Chair or Writing Chair: these terms are applied indifferently to the following two distinct types, both of which appeared in the first quarter of the 18th century. (*a*) An armchair with three uprights in the back, one placed centrally with a separate splat on each side, and the four legs arranged so that one was in the centre of a projecting angle in the front seat-rail and another opposite to it at the rear, below the central upright. Either of the splats could be leaned against, and the user's tablet or book could be rested on one of the level arms. (*b*) An upholstered chair with a back which narrowed at the base and was often surmounted by a sloping wooden rest between two padded horizontal supports. This type, which is sometimes miscalled a 'cock-fighting chair',

Reading Chairs

could be used in the normal manner, or could be sat upon astride with the user's arms resting on the supports.

Reeding: carved decoration occurring on legs, etc., of furniture chiefly in the late 18th and early 19th centuries, and consisting of parallel beads, of approximately semicircular section, named by analogy with reeds laid side by side. Reeding became more popular than fluting (*q.v.*) at the time in question. During the Regency period it often occurred on the upper surface of chair-arms as well as on legs.

Refectory Table: a modern name for a large table of fixed construction, as opposed to a trestle-table, prevalent from the mid-16th century to after 1660 and usually made of oak. The ancestors of the type were found sparsely in the middle ages when they were known as 'dormant tables', and there is no evidence that they originated in monastic houses.

Regency Style: the historic Regency began in 1811, when George III's insanity made it impossible for him to discharge his duties, and ended in 1820 when he died and the Regent, George, Prince of Wales, ascended the throne as George IV. As a term denoting a style, however, 'Regency' is concerned with a much longer period beginning in the last years of the 18th century and

Regency Couch or Settee

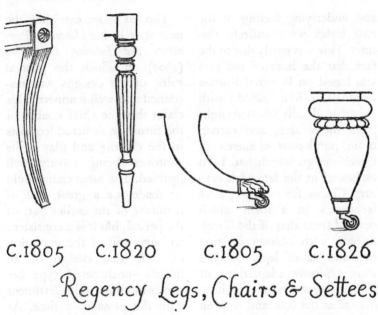

c.1805   c.1820   c.1805   c.1826

Regency Legs, Chairs & Settees

ending in about 1830, after which, in the reign of William IV, taste began to be overwhelmed by the pronounced decadence which was to characterise most of the Victorian era. After the outbreak of the Revolution, while France was being governed by the Directory (*Directoire*), French taste turned towards a severe classical manner which was interpreted and transformed in England by Henry Holland (*q.v.*). In this may be seen the beginnings of the Regency style, which attained full maturity in the early 19th century under

the influence of Thomas Hope (*q.v.*) and Sir John Soane.

Whereas exponents of the Adam style had freely adapted classical forms and ornament to accord with the prevailing desire for lightness and elegance, the new style represented a striving for archaeological exactitude which was not always attainable in a strict sense as designers were often dealing with objects which had never existed in classical times. Though there were frequent correspondences between ornamental details of the Adam and Regency periods, the aspect

121

and underlying feeling of the two styles were entirely distinct. This was partly due to the fact that the later of the two was based on Imperial Roman originals, often allied with Egyptian details taken straight from the source, and certain more ponderous elements of Greek design which had been eschewed in the late 18th century. Chairs, for example, were frequently in a form which derived from that of the Greek *klismos*, with oblong cresting rails and 'sabre' legs. Couches were typically adaptations of Roman prototypes, scrolling inward at the foot and with an outward roll to the head, while the legs were either of 'sabre' form or consisted of animal legs surmounted by lions' heads.

Various kinds of applied metal enrichment, usually gilt, achieved great popularity and produced a striking tonal contrast against backgrounds of darker wood. Brass inlay, in the form of stringing or conventionalised floral and foliate motifs, was widely used and was particularly effective in association with rosewood, which increasingly usurped the position of satinwood in important rooms.

Thomas Hope exhibited the new style in his *Household Furniture and Interior Decoration* (1807), in which the general spirit of the designs was restrained and well-mannered, his claim that the chief quality of the furniture depicted 'consists in the chastity and play of its contours' being mostly well justified. The same claim could be made for a great deal of furniture of the earlier part of the period, but it is a consistent characteristic of the evolution of style that design of an initially uncluttered type becomes modified to its detriment with the passage of time. As the 19th century advanced into its second quarter the forms and decoration of much furniture became increasingly coarsened, so that the approaching decline was inevitable. Regency was the last of the great traditional styles, and there is some truth in the suggestion that design has been floundering ever since.

Renaissance: the rebirth of the classical spirit which began in Italy to supersede the Gothic, which was a northern importation, in about the middle of the 15th century. The resultant style, which was based on tradition and such original classical buildings as still remained standing, spread through the Habsburg empire and the duchy of Burgundy to arrive in England in the early 16th century. In view of the channel by which it arrived, it is not surprising that renaissance ornament in England should have had a strongly Germanic flavour for most of the 16th century. Although the acceptance of the style was probably facilitated by the arrival in England in 1526 of the Augsburg artist Hans Holbein the Younger, who was a gifted designer as well as a painter, Gothic influence lingered on until about the middle of the century. Even thereafter, despite the widespread use of renaissance motifs, the plethoric character of carved decoration showed that popular taste was still under the spell of the Gothic architectural spirit, and this resulted in a kind of burlesque of the renaissance style which persisted well into the 17th century. However, the decorative elements of the style owed nothing to Gothic architecture as in the previous period, and consisted of classical heads in medallions (Romayne heads),

acanthus leaves, gadroons, guilloche, fluting (q.q.v.), round-headed arches, trophies of Roman armour, female terminal figures developing, below their navels, into foliate scrollwork, etc.

In the second half of the 17th century twist-turning was introduced from France. It was sometimes used in renaissance architecture for columns, for example, those supporting Bernini's baldachin over the high altar in St. Peter's, Rome. In the reign of Charles II, when this form of turning was most prevalent, ornament, especially on chairs, was over-elaborate though skilfully executed, but became muted in the last decade of the century. This more modest rendering of the renaissance manner continued after 1700 in the different idiom of the Queen Anne period, with furniture owing more to its satisfying forms and proportions than to decoration.

The last fling of the renaissance style was in the English version of baroque, restrained in comparison with its Continental equivalent but nevertheless making use of florid and sometimes overpowering ornament such as heavy swags, scallop shells, writhing scrolls, paw feet, eagles' heads and heavy architectural details with the appearance of wood-coloured masonry (see William Kent). This style began to be superseded by rococo (*q.v.*) in the 1740s, but certain architectural details of renaissance origin, such as pediments, persisted all through the Chippendale period until they gained renewed authority in the neoclassical phase inaugurated chiefly by Robert Adam (*q.v.*).

Rent-Table: a term of uncertain validity applied to a type of table, made from about 1750 until the early 19th century, having a circular or polygonal top with usually seven drawers in the frieze often labelled with the days of the week. Another type had concealed compartments in the top, which sometimes rotated on the underframe.

Ribband-Back Chair: a mahogany chair, which began to be made in England in the mid-18th century, with a back containing ribbons and bows carved in profile and relief with much realism. In the *Director* Chippendale (*q.v.*) illustrated examples of which he was very proud and of which he said

Ribband-Back
(Chippendale)

'they are the best I have ever seen', though the design, which involved the use of cross-grained wood in the horizontal parts, was unsound mechanically. Surviving specimens are of the utmost rarity owing, probably, to the high rate of destruction and the likelihood that very few sets were made, the carving of the backs demanding a degree of skill which could not have been generally available.

Rocaille: a French name for rococo (*q.v.*).

Rococo: a French colloquial

term of the early 19th century originally meaning freakish or extravagant. It came into use in England in about 1830 and was accepted thereafter in both countries as an equivalent of *rocaille*. This was a lively ornamental style evolved in Paris in the 1720s by a group of architects including Meissonnier, as a rebellious reaction against the heavy smugness of French baroque. It was characterised by broken scrolls, formalised rock and shell motifs, and floral and foliate sprays which were usually asymmetrical. It was often of such a fortuitous and dynamic aspect that it gave a superficial impression of imminent disintegration, but in fact was conceived with such skill that a feeling of balance was somehow achieved. Louis XV issued a *lettre de cachet* ordering the Paris goldsmiths to admit Meissonnier to their guild, and thereafter rococo design spread over the entire field of applied art including furniture. In England, Matthias Lock (*q.v.*) was one of its earliest pioneers and began to produce ornamental designs in the new style in 1740, but it gained almost universal recognition when Chippendale published his *Director* in 1754,

owing to the wide circulation which the work achieved. Mingled with Chinese and 'Gothick' elements it remained fashionable until about 1765, after which, although it still persisted here and there particularly in the provinces, it was generally replaced by the neo-classical style. In England, it was known throughout the period of its currency as the 'modern' style. See Girandole.

Roentgen, Abraham: a celebrated German cabinet-maker who practised his craft in England for some years in the second quarter of the 18th century. In Germany, in the middle of the century, he popularised the English style, some of his work being based on designs in Chippendale's *Director*. His more famous son David, who made a great deal of furniture for export to France, described himself as an 'English Cabinet-maker'.

Romayne Heads: carved heads in roundels, which often consisted of wreaths of bay leaves, used as relief ornament on English oak furniture in the first half of the 16th century and sometimes on wall-panelling. The heads were usually in profile and were of either men or women, the former being mostly warriors wearing helmets of vaguely classical appearance very like the contemporary burgonet. These medallions derived from renaissance architectural motifs used in Italy from about 1450; a number appear on the façade of the Certosa at Pavia. See Chest or Coffer.

Rope-Back Chair: a modern descriptive term sometimes applied to an early 19th-century chair with one of the crossrails in the back carved in the form of rope.

Rosewood: a hard, dark timber imported chiefly from the East Indies and Brazil. It was used sparsely for inlay in the 17th century and more often for banding, etc., in the 18th century. After 1800 it became immensely popular and was frequently used in the form of veneer and occasionally in the solid. It looked particularly effective in association with gilt or brass enrichment, and its prestige was so great that many chairs of the period were made of beech grained and darkened in imitation. It gained its name from its pleasant odour when cut.

Runners: a term sometimes used to denote the wooden strips along the sides of drawers, but more familiar as sliding members working through slots or apertures of rectangular section. Among these may be mentioned the pairs of long runners attached to the leaves of draw-tables in the 16th and 17th centuries, and the pull-out supports for the falls of bureaux, tops of bachelors' chests, etc. From the late 17th century these were usually called 'Lopers' by cabinet-makers.

S

Sabicu: a central American timber having something of the appearance of mahogany but brown rather than red in colour. It was used to some extent for banding in the second half of the 18th century, and for veneer during the Regency period.

Sabre Leg: also known as a Scimitar Leg. A concave, forward-curving leg used especially on chairs in the early 19th century and deriving from a member of similar shape on an ancient Greek chair, the *klismos*. Some early examples were exactly like the classical originals and projected well forward, but as it was soon discovered that, in this form, they constituted an inconvenient obstacle and were liable to be galled by the feet of the sitter, they were made to curve inward so that the base of the leg was in a perpendicular line with the front of the seat-rail. They were either of rectangular section, often reeded, or rounded in front. Sabre legs occurred on tables, sideboards, etc., as well as on chairs and settees. They continued after 1830 alongside the straight, turned legs which had regained their original popularity shortly before 1820.

Saddle Seat: a popular name for the type of curved 18th-century chair-seat with the centre lower than the sides.

Sand-Burning: a method of obtaining effects of shading in marquetry.

Satinwood: a brownish yellow timber imported into Britain from the East Indies and West Indies and used for furniture of high quality in the second half of the 18th century. Being an expensive wood it was seldom employed in the solid, but was often used as banding on mahogany furniture and in the form of veneer for cabinets, the tops of Pembroke tables, etc. The West Indian variety was preferred as it had a better figure in the grain and was available in wider planks. Sheraton considered satinwood to be the finest of all timbers.

Scagliola: a composition of Roman origin consisting of a hard plaster containing inset pieces of variously coloured marbles, alabaster, porphyry, etc., usually arranged in formal patterns. The technique was revived in Italy in the early 17th century, and although scagliola seems to have been made to some extent in the Netherlands, probably by immigrant craftsmen, Florence enjoyed a virtual monopoly until the second half of the 18th century. The earliest example in England appears to be an Italian fire-place surround at Ham House dating from about 1670, but in the first quarter of the 18th century scagliola began to be more widely used for the tops of elaborately carved side-tables which were often gilt. From about 1730 it was fashionable for the tops of commodes (*q.v.*) of the highest quality, and continued to be used for this purpose throughout the 18th century. From about 1760 it began to be made in London by a firm named Richter and Bartoli, whose productions enjoyed a high reputation, but some no doubt

continued to be imported from Italy as well.

Scratch Carving: a perfunctory method of carving on furniture of the 16th and 17th centuries in which the pattern was formed by thin, incised lines. It was a less laborious, though less effective, method than removing the ground to leave the motifs in relief.

Screen Desk: a late 18th-century combination of a small

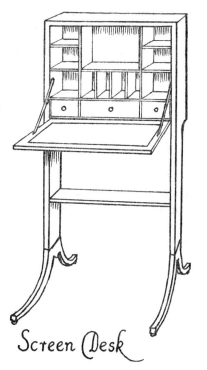

Screen Desk

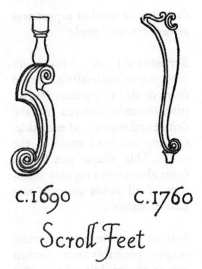

c.1690   c.1760

Scroll Feet

fire-screen mounted on two up-rights having a fall front for writing. Thomas Shearer (*q.v.*) illustrated a 'Lady's Writing Fire Screen' in 1788.

Scriptor: see Scrutoir.

Scroll Foot: a terminal to a furniture leg consisting of an outward-curving volute, oc-curring first in the late 17th century in strongly-emphasised form, then in reduced size, with usually a downward extension beneath, from the mid-18th century on cabriole legs. This type was often associated with chairs and settees of French inspiration.

Scrutoir: a late 17th-century

English corruption of the French term *escritoire* used to describe a writing cabinet, mounted either on a stand or a chest of drawers, with a front panel, hinged at the base, which could be lowered to a horizontal position where it was supported by chains or metal elbows.

Seat Rails: the four horizontal rails supporting the seat of a chair or settee.

Secretaire: a variant of the 18th-century term 'secretary' and now often applied to a writing-cabinet with a baize-covered surface in the top drawer to distinguish the type from an ordinary bureau. Sher-aton applied the word to what is more often called a Carlton House Table (*q.v.*).

Secretaire

Seddon, George: a celebrated London cabinet-maker from about 1750 who was described in the *Annual Register* of 1768 as 'one of the most eminent cabinet-makers of London'. He died in 1801 but the firm continued in operation until the mid-19th century, enjoying always a consistently high reputation. Little surviving furniture can be identified with it but it was evidently a vast undertaking, the value of its stock in 1789 being almost £120,000, an immense sum in those days. From the diary of Sophie von la Roche (*Tagebuch einer Reise durch Holland und England . . .*), who saw the firm's premises in 1788, a number of interesting facts emerge: four hundred craftsmen of various kinds were employed apart from apprentices, including carvers, gilders, upholsterers, mirror-makers, locksmiths and workers in ormolu (*q.v.*). Seddon was a designer as well as a manufacturer, and his productions ranged from the 'simplest to the most elegant'. This last comment is of great significance, for since it implies that a large-scale manufacturer catered for all sections of the trade, it tends to upset the commonly-held opinion that

furniture of modest aspect was always country-made.

Serpentine: an 18th-century term for an undulating, curved front or side to a piece of furniture, usually convex at the centre and concave at each side, curving outward again at the ends. This shape was found from about 1750 on case furniture of all kinds and the seat rails of chairs.

Settee: a term of uncertain origin, probably not current before the middle of the 18th century, used retrospectively to denote a seat for two or more persons, upholstered or otherwise rendered more comfortable or elegant than a settle (*q.v.*). The upholstered variant was probably introduced about 1600, and examples differing somewhat in principle have survived from the early 17th century, notably at Knole Park in Kent. One was of fixed construction like most later types, while the other, often called a 'Knole Settee', had wings which could be let down to make it more convenient for reclining and so convert it into a day-bed (*q.v.*). Soon after the middle of the 17th century the chair-back settee was introduced, and despite its limited comfort continued to be made far into the 19th century. Apart from an obvious affinity between this type of settee and contemporary chairs, upholstered varieties also displayed similarities of detail with their smaller counterparts in the way of legs, arms, etc. A familiarity with the design of chairs will therefore enable settees also to be assigned to their proper periods.

Settle: a wooden seat with back and arms to accommodate several persons, which may have developed from the chest, the most widely-distributed piece of furniture in the middle ages. Medieval examples were of two main kinds: a readily movable type with open or panelled back and sometimes provided with a foot-board to avoid draughts, and a box-settle with hinged seat consisting, in effect, of a chest with back-rest and an arm at each end. Both types continued in domestic surroundings into the second half of the 17th century, and less frequently in the 18th century when they were usually confined to taverns. Settles were almost invariably made of oak. A rare 17th-century variety had, in addition to

Settle c.1640

the box-seat, a shallow cupboard in the high back which is usually considered as being for the storage of bacon. In the Georgian period, mahogany hall seats wholly of wood were made in all the succeeding styles, but apart from the lack of upholstery they were entirely similar to settees, from which they were distinguished chiefly by their extreme discomfort.

Settle-Table: see Table-Settle.

Sewing-Table: see Work-Table.

Shearer, Thomas: a distinguished designer and cabinet-maker of the late 18th century, author of many of the illustrations in the *Cabinet Maker's London Book of Prices* (first published in 1788 with further editions in 1793, 1805 and 1823), most of the others being by George Hepplewhite. It was essentially a practical work which divided the prices into costs of material and workmanship. In the year of the first edition, Shearer published those designs for which he had been responsible in *Designs for Household Furniture* under his own name. These included well-drawn and ingenious pieces

such as dressing-tables with all manner of internal contrivances including, in accordance with contemporary requirements, facilities for writing. He was the first designer to illustrate a hybrid version of the two existing types of sideboard (*q.v.*), in which the self-contained variety, with drawers and cellaret, was attached to urn-crowned pedestals. Sheraton (*q.v.*) made use of the idea in his *Drawing Book* (1791–1794).

Shelves: unenclosed tiers of boards for the accommodation of books, plate, pottery and other things have been known since the medieval period, but did not appear in the English domestic scene with any regularity until the early 17th century. They were either of the hanging variety, suspended from the wall, or were free-standing, supported on feet which rested on the floor. Oak examples have survived from the Jacobean era, and were usually carved on the cresting in typical fashion with lunettes, guilloche, etc. The frames were mostly in the form of paired round-headed arches such as were found on panelling, chests and chair-backs at the same time, but unless the piece was unusually wide, the arches sprang, in the centre, from a short pendant rather than a pillar or pilaster which would have interrupted the shelf space. The incidence of hanging shelves greatly increased in the early 18th century with the growing vogue for collecting Oriental ceramics which had begun in the 17th century; but it seems to have waned until the middle of the century, possibly owing to the popularity of cabinets on bureaux, which served the same purpose.

In the 1750s, hanging or standing shelves in the Chinese taste became noticeably prevalent, the ends being often fretted with an open diagonal cross embodying a swastika—an ancient Chinese emblem—formed at the central intersection. This kind of fretting, which had an obvious affinity with the Oriental porcelain which often stood on the shelves, continued even into the neo-classical period with which it was basically incongruous; but this was an age of intelligent compromise, and one may recall the commodes of the same period with chinoiserie panels which equally lacked counterparts in ancient Greece and Rome. Hepplewhite illustrated chinoiserie shelves in his *Guide* which was otherwise devoted to a popular rendering of the neo-classical manner. In the last decade of the 18th century, when turned supports were becoming frequent on other types of furniture, they also appeared on hanging shelves, the vertical pillars being often surmounted by small urns. In the Regency period, open pendant shelves continued to be made, and were sometimes inlaid with brass like other contemporary furniture.

Shepherd's Crook Arm: a descriptive term applied to the arm of a chair or settee with the angle between the horizontal rest and the upright curved like a shepherd's crook, popular in the early 18th century on walnut furniture. The same formation often occurred at the

Shepherd's Crook Arm

angle between the uprights and cresting-rail of chairs in the Queen Anne period.

Sheraton, Thomas (1751-1806): the most celebrated designer of the last decade of the 18th century. He was born at Stockton-on-Tees and had many years of experience as a practical cabinet-maker in someone else's employ, when he no doubt found an outlet for his 'strong attachment and inclination for carving'. He came to London in about 1790 and between 1791 and 1794 published *The Cabinet-Maker's and Upholsterer's Drawing Book* in four parts. Although the designs of both Hepplewhite (*q.v.*) and Sheraton were conceived as a modified rendering of the neo-classical style, and their publication was separated by only three years, they display noticeable differences in feeling. Both authors were careful to keep their designs within the framework of the prevailing taste which had not yet run its course, but Sheraton was more imaginative and adventurous than his predecessor even if the results were at times less satisfactory.

He drew part of his inspiration from the France of Louis XVI, and this manifested itself in a number of ways including the provision of brass galleries round the edges of some flat surfaces, tiers of small shelves of roughly triangular shape

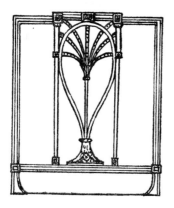 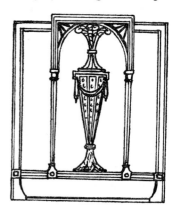

Sheraton Chair-Backs

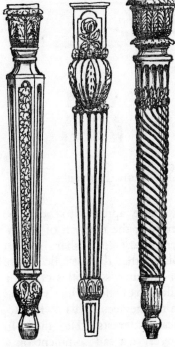

Sheraton Chair-Legs

Pembroke tables, which were much better in the existing style with four tapering legs.

In regard to chairs, Sheraton's designs displayed an apparent flimsiness of detail which was, however, usually belied in specimens actually executed. These were not only elegant and refined but also sufficiently strong for civilised use. Most of his chair-backs were rectangular in accordance with late 18th-century taste, but he illustrated a few shield-backs in which the usual convex, central part of the cresting-rail was partly replaced by a horizontal portion.

In 1803, Sheraton published an illustrated *Cabinet Dictionary* containing designs of high quality, often in an inchoate version of the style now known

contrived in the ends of cabinets and sideboards, and the rather unfortunate use of spiral reeding and grooving on legs. He was also attached to pillar-and-claw supports—a constructional mannerism which gained ground in the early 19th century—and although this was eminently satisfactory on certain objects such as work-tables, it produced an ill-balanced effect when applied to

Sheraton 'Kidney Table'

as 'Regency', but devoid of the excesses which were to appear later. His final publication was one volume of a grandiose work entitled the *Cabinet-Maker, Upholsterer, and General Artist's Encyclopaedia*, issued in 1805. It included pieces in the Regency style but also afforded evidence of a pathological mental state.

The most important of all these was undoubtedly the *Drawing Book*, which was subscribed by nearly six hundred cabinet-makers and associated craftsmen in various parts of the country and exercised a profound influence on contemporary design. Many pieces of furniture surviving from the period are obviously based with varying degrees of fidelity on his illustrations, but it must be remembered that the adjective 'Sheraton' is a mere generic term as in the case of Chippendale and Hepplewhite and does not indicate that a piece so described was actually made by Sheraton. There seems no doubt that he never had a cabinet-making business of his own, for the trade card which he used after settling in London mentioned his activities as a designer and a teacher of drawing, etc., but said nothing of cabinet-making.

Sheraton Pembroke Table

There appears to be some truth in the opinion of a contemporary publisher (Adam Black) that the catholic nature of Sheraton's abilities caused a dilution of effort which resulted in the neglect of his own practical interests. He died in poverty: a sad comment on a society which, while content to exploit the inventions of a genius, was also willing to let him starve.

Sheveret: see Cheveret.

Shield-Back: a chair- or settee-back of the second half of the 18th century with the splat contained in a shield-shaped surround. The base of such a back was raised above the level of the seat and was usually rounded but sometimes pointed. The style is associated with

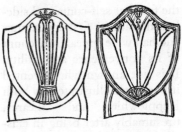

Shield-Backs

the name of Hepplewhite but was not his invention.

Shoe: a shaped piece of wood attached to the top of the rear seat-rails of chairs after 1700 to hold the base of the splat. Its use was not universal, the splat sometimes being slotted directly into the seat-rail, but was widely current on chairs of good quality and appropriate construction. It was unnecessary in the late 17th century because the back-rest of the chair did not then make contact with the rear seat-rail, and was naturally not found on later examples, such as shield-back chairs, in which there was also a space below the back, between the uprights.

Sideboard: literally, a side-table, but assuming a special status through being sited, from the early 18th century, in the dining-room where it was used in the serving of meals. Even some of the earliest had marble or scagliola (q.v.) tops and were generally distinguished from side-tables in other parts of a house only by their situation. Chippendale (q.v.) applied the name 'sideboard tables' to designs illustrated in the *Director*—a tautological term used presumably to emphasise the connection with meals. These tables were mostly of heavy construction and often displayed ornament of Chinese or rococo type, usually in combination.

Robert Adam (q.v.) produced a number of more elegant designs in the neo-classical manner and enhanced the usefulness of the piece by providing a pedestal at each end, of the same height as the table,

Sideboard (Hepplewhite)

137

surmounted by an urn which was used as a container for water or as a knife-case. Urns intended to contain water generally had taps in the base. The pedestals, mostly of square section, were used for storage of dining-room accessories, for which there had previously been no provision, and one of the pair sometimes embodied a tin-lined plate-warmer. Sideboards of this kind formed a balanced and imposing composition, and continued to be used in larger houses where space was of no consideration well into the Regency period, undergoing the characteristic changes which occurred on other furniture. A wine-cooler was often sited underneath.

In the last quarter of the 18th century, when modified versions of the original neo-classical style were in general use,

the familiar self-contained sideboard made its first appearance and had wide appeal on account of its convenience and utility. It is not known who invented it but it was illustrated by both Hepplewhite and Shearer, presumably after being in existence for some years. It was mounted on legs and had a shallow drawer in the frieze for cutlery and flatware, and a deeper cupboard or drawer at each side, one of which contained a metal-lined cellaret for bottles. Shearer devised a hybrid of this and the existing type by attaching pedestals at the ends. A feature sometimes occurring in the late 18th century was a small cupboard at one end to contain a chamberpot—a refinement which provides a curious comment on Georgian dining-room habits. From quite soon after their introduction many of these sideboards had open brass-rod superstructures fixed at the rear of the tops, sometimes embodying a horizontal rail to support a short, ruched curtain. It is recorded that the purpose of these brass superstructures was 'to support large dishes', though if this meant that the dishes were stood on end and leaned against the rails, the

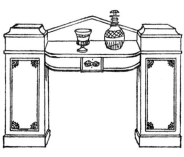

Sideboard (Regency)

arrangement seems rather precarious, as there is no evidence that any sort of ridge was provided to prevent the dishes slipping down. From the last decade of the 18th century the space below the central frieze might contain a shelf, usually concealed behind a tambour (*q.v.*) working from side to side, and this feature persisted into the early 19th century.

Although the general design of the late 18th-century sideboard was widely retained after 1800, modified by the presence of Regency ornament and the various kinds of legs found on other furniture at the same time, a popular form was basically different in conception. This type comprised a horizontal platform, with the usual shallow drawer or drawers in the frieze, supported by a tall pedestal at each end containing drawers and cupboards. The bases of the pedestals rested commonly on low plinths or small gadrooned ball-feet. Above the rear of the top a low, vertical board, extending the whole length, often rose in the shape of a triangular pediment and this, combined with the solid pedestals extending almost to the floor, was liable to give these Regency

sideboards a heavy architectural character which, while wholly consonant with the stylistic spirit of the age, was greatly at variance with the lighter elegance of the Adam period.

Silver Table: see China Table.

Silverwood: probably a synonym in the 18th century for harewood (*q.v.*).

Slat: a thin bar of wood, such as the cross-rails in a ladder-back chair. In America these were often called 'Slat-back chairs'.

Smith, George: designer, cabinet-maker and upholsterer who worked for the Prince of Wales before and after his accession as George IV. In 1808 he published *A Collection of Designs for Household Furniture and Interior Decoration*, containing elements of the Greek, Roman and Egyptian styles together with Gothic and Chinese. In 1812 he issued a *Collection of Ornamental Designs after the Manner of the Antique* and in 1826 appeared his *Cabinet-Makers' and Upholsterers' Guide, Drawing Book, and Repository of New and Original Designs for Household Furniture*: a title as unwieldy as some of the designs contained in it, and whose choice seems to suggest that now that Hepplewhite's and Sheraton's chief designs were consigned to limbo, his own represented the last word in merit. Apparently Smith received a great deal of distinguished patronage as a cabinet-maker, though many of the details of his designs were clumsy and ill-proportioned. See Tea Poy.

Sofa Table c.1795

Sofa: a term deriving from the Arabic *suffah*, a bench, almost indistinguishable in English usage from 'settee', but usually implying a seat which was not only capable of seating several persons but was also large enough for one to recline on. The word was probably introduced into English in the late 17th century and was used thereafter by Chippendale and others in relation to upholstered pieces.

Sofa Table: a rectangular table, introduced in the late 18th century, whose general dimensions, according to Sheraton, were between 5 ft. and 6 ft. long and from 22 in. to 24 in. wide. The tops were sometimes fixed but more usually had hinged flaps at the ends supported on fly brackets which

swung out from the framework. The earliest supports consisted of end-standards with two curved legs branching out from the base of each. Straight or curved stretchers united the standards just below the tops and were almost out of sight, but in the early 19th century turned stretchers usually ran between the bases of the standards just above the legs, or the top rested on some kind of central support. These tables

Sofa Table c.1810

were commonly situated in front of sofas though they were sometimes placed behind them, and were chiefly for the use of ladies. The frieze of a sofa table contained two drawers with false drawer-fronts on the opposite side.

Spade Foot: a downward-tapering, usually square-section foot on the legs of furniture in the late 18th century, possibly deriving from a classical pedestal; known also as a Therm foot. See Chairs and Sideboards.

Spandrel: an architectural term applied to furniture and indicating the roughly triangular space between the curving top side of an arch and the rectangular frame containing it, or the space between the tops of two arches.

Spanish Foot: a terminal which first appeared on legged furniture in the last decade of the 17th century and consisting of a carved scroll with vertical channels or ribs, somewhat suggestive of a hand resting on a flat surface with the fingers doubled inward. It persisted to some extent into the early 18th century, usually, however, ac-

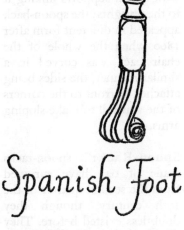

Spanish Foot

companied by other details which indicate the period. It is also known as the Braganza foot.

Splat or Splad: the chief vertical member or members within the framework of a chairback.

Split-Turning: a decorative moulding formed by turning a piece of wood and dividing it down the centre to provide two identical portions; applied as ornament to oak furniture from about 1600.

Spoon-Back: a wooden chairback occurring in the early 18th century, with the main part of the splat shaped in a hollow curve from side to side, usually with lateral supports linking it to the uprights; the spoon-back appeared in different form after 1800 when the whole of the chair back was curved in a similar manner, the sides being attached in front to the corners of the seat-rail to make sloping arms.

Spoon-Rack: spoon-racks made of oak have survived from the second quarter of the 17th century, though they doubtless existed before. They usually consisted of a rear board of thin wood with a shaped cresting, below which was a narrow shelf pierced with a row of holes. Through

Spoon-Back Chair c.1815

these, contemporary pewter spoons with fig-shaped bowls and small finials were suspended bowl-upwards. A cutlery-box, with or without a hinged lid, was attached to the base of the rear board. After 1660 the holes for the stems of the spoons became wider, to permit the passage of the trifid finials then in vogue. This design continued with little variation through the 18th century together with another type, introduced after 1700, with several pierced racks arranged like steps. The dating of these objects is generally very difficult and one can seldom do more than assign them to their proper century. Some assistance is given by the fact that 17th-century examples were often slightly carved in a manner typical of the period.

Squab: a shaped cushion which rests on a piece of seating furniture but is not permanently attached to it. The term probably first came into use in the first half of the 17th century as an extended use of an adjective spelt in the same manner meaning short and fat. Some chair seats of the mid-17th century were dished to take a squab. See Derbyshire Chair.

Standard: a name given to large chests in the medieval period and the 16th century, sometimes used for the storage of armour.

Stile: the outside vertical part of the framework of a chest, cabinet, etc. See also Muntin.

Stirrup-Cup Table: an uncommon type of small occasional table in mahogany or rosewood, introduced in the early 19th century, similar in appearance to the largest table

Stirrup-Cup Table

of a quartetto (*q.v.*) nest, but having a narrow pull-out shelf on each side pierced with a row of holes. These accommodated the stems of the footless glasses, similar to coaching glasses, used to serve liquor at a 'lawn meet' to huntsmen in the saddle.

Stool: a term now applied only to a seat without back or arms for one person or several, but originally used in a wider sense. In the middle ages, one of the commonest types of stool in western Europe had three vertical legs, either cut or turned, and a triangular top of planking or rushes. Such stools are frequently shown in contemporary paintings and manuscript illuminations. Later, one of the legs was prolonged upwards to form a back rest (see Back-Stool) and this formed the basis of many turned chairs with triangular seats which continued to be made until the second quarter of the 17th century.

In the 15th century the so-called slab-ended stool appeared. It was supported, not on legs, but on end-standards consisting of short lengths of oak plank with a Gothic arch cut out of the base of each. The outer edges of these 'slab ends'

Stool, Slab-Ended

were shaped to look like architectural buttresses. Deep rails, often with shallow pointed or ogival arches, ran below the edges of the top and were slotted through the ends, the whole being held together with iron nails. Sometimes, an independent stretcher linked the supports, emerging through a hole at each end where it was retained in position by a wedge driven through a shaped aperture. These stools continued through the first half of the 16th century, gradually losing their Gothic architectural details, and were then superseded by the joined stool (*q.v.*). Thereafter, stools were similar in appearance to the lower parts of contemporary chairs

and may always be broadly dated by analogy with them, the only difference being that all four legs were of the same design, since there was no back or front.

Strapwork: renaissance ornament, found on oak furniture in the late 16th and 17th centuries, consisting of parallel-sided ribbons carved in relief, often allied with flowers, foliage and scrolls. The term is also applied to the shapes produced by piercing the splats of chairs from about 1740 to the end of the Chippendale period.

Straw-Work: the embellishment of furniture by sticking variously-coloured split straws on the surface with an effect similar to that of marquetry. The technique was used with great skill in Italy in the first half of the 17th century, and English examples have survived from the time of Charles II to the early 19th century, Dunstable in Bedfordshire being the chief centre of production. Excellent work of this kind was done by French prisoners in England during the Napoleonic wars.

Stretchers: wooden bars of

various shapes uniting the legs of chairs, stools, settees, stands, etc.

Stringing: inlaid lines on furniture in various materials including wood, ivory or metal.

Stuart, James (1713–1788): a prominent architect known as 'Athenian Stuart' owing to his joint authorship of the first volume of *Antiquities of Athens*, which was published in 1762 and was based largely on his studies of classical art made during a visit to Greece from which he returned in 1755. The second and third volumes were published posthumously in 1788 and 1795 respectively. He designed or altered a number of notable houses and sometimes the furniture for them, and would doubtless have achieved even more in the practical sphere had it not been for his lazy temperament. As a protagonist of the neo-classical style he was overshadowed by his contemporary, Robert Adam, but the latter paid courteous and justified tribute to the contribution he made 'towards introducing the true style of antique decoration'.

Stump: the vertical support

for the arm of a chair, its base being attached to the seat-rail.

Sunburst: inlaid semicircular motif containing rays, sometimes used at the bases of cabinets in the early 18th century, and often set in a concave lunette.

Supper Table: a name given from about 1740 to a type of claw table (*q.v.*) with closely-spaced circular recesses on the top to hold small plates for an informal collation last thing at night.

Swag: a drooping festoon of classical origin used during the renaissance and again in the classical-revival period, when it consisted chiefly of husks, flowers, leaves or simulated cloth.

Sycamore: a kind of maple yielding a timber varying from white to yellow, and sometimes brown in old trees. It was used to some extent for marquetry in the late 17th and early 18th centuries and on a considerable scale during the Adam period both in the solid and as veneer, the latter being sometimes in the form of harewood (*q.v.*).

T

Table-Chair: a composite piece of furniture introduced in the late 15th century consisting of a chair with hinged back which swung over and rested on the arms. Most surviving examples are of 17th-century origin, but there are some modern reproductions.

Table-Settle: similar in principle to a table-chair, but comprising a settle with a hinged back which, when folded over to rest on the arms at each end, formed a narrow table wider and longer than the settle, which usually had a box-seat. Most existing specimens date from the middle decades of the 17th century, when they must have been very much more popular than before. They are sometimes described by the unfortunate modern jargon term 'monks' benches', though the vast majority were made at least a hundred years after the dissolution of the monasteries.

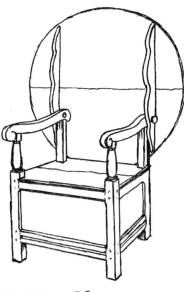

Table-Chair c.1650

Tallboy: a double chest of drawers, with one standing upon the other, introduced at the end of the 17th century when it was known as a 'chest-upon-chest'. The term 'tallboy', which manifestly began as a colloquialism, attained respectability in the last quarter of the 18th century owing to its greater convenience and was used by Hepplewhite in the *Guide*.

Early examples sometimes had arc-shaped hoods above the cornices like some contemporary bureau-bookcases and bureau-cabinets and were occasionally japanned. From the early 18th century, however, most were of polished walnut surmounted by straight, concave cornices, the corners of the upper chest being frequently canted, while the base of the front might be inlaid with a sunburst (*q.v.*). After the introduction of mahogany tallboys also began to be made of this timber, though walnut continued popular in this connection after it had become generally outmoded on other furniture. From the Queen Anne period onwards, the top of the lower chest sometimes contained a secretaire drawer. The use of tallboys was by no means confined to bed-chambers.

Tambour: a flexible form of closure consisting of narrow strips of wood glued to a textile base and familiar on the roll-top desk. Tambours were introduced from France where they had been in use since about 1750, and were chiefly popular in England in the last quarter of the 18th century. They were used for many minor purposes in connection, for example, with night-tables (*q.v.*) and sideboards, but were particularly attractive on cylinder-desks (*q.v.*). The writing surface of such a desk normally had quadrant-shaped sides, and a groove, following the shape of the edge, was cut in each of these to take the ends of the tambour which, when opened or closed, travelled along a curving path. Tambours continued to be used in the early 19th century, but it must have been discovered that their inherent fragility made them vulnerable to pressure, and Sheraton, in his *Cabinet Dictionary* of 1803, said that they were 'almost out of use being both insecure and liable to injury'.

Tatham, Charles Heathcote (1772–1842): an architect and sometime pupil of Henry Holland (*q.v.*), who had great influence on early 19th-century design especially in regard to furniture and silver. He maintained that the principal characteristic of the latter should be massiveness: a quality which was increasingly displayed in furniture also as the Regency style gained momentum. He had travelled extensively in Italy for several years in the late 18th century, and published a collection of etchings of classical architecture. A further collection illustrating Grecian and Roman architectural details appeared in 1806. His designs were widely drawn upon by contemporary cabinet-makers.

Tatham, Thomas (1763–1818): elder brother of Charles Heathcote Tatham and partner from about 1800 of the well-known cabinet-maker and upholsterer, William Marsh (*q.v.*). A canopied bed designed by Tatham is still in use at Powderham Castle, Devon.

Tea Caddy: an English corruption of a Malay word, *kati*, which denoted a weight equivalent to about a pound and a quarter. In the late 18th century it came to mean a container for tea rather than a quantity, and superseded the existing phrases 'tea-chest' and 'tea-canister'. The terms were often used loosely, but strictly speaking, a canister was a smaller container kept in the chest. Caddies varied in their internal arrangements. Some might contain canisters of silver, base metal or glass, others might be divided into compartments by partitions, while

small specimens were sometimes designed for one kind of tea only. Early examples are rare, but more have survived from the middle of the 18th century and especially from the Adam period, when they were mostly of rectangular or oval shape, and often decorated with painted or inlaid ornament. In the Regency period, they were more usually of casket-form, mounted on metal feet in the prevailing style.

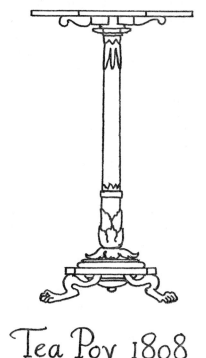

Tea Poy 1808

Tea Poy: originally, a small table of any kind particularly the tripod variety. The word derives from the Hindustani *tipai,* and had no essential relationship with tea, but since small tables were commonly used in this connection, the sense eventually became altered in the 19th century to accord with the corrupt English spelling. In his *Household Furniture* of 1808, George Smith (*q.v.*) illustrated a design for a tea poy which merely consisted of a small table on pillar-and-claw support. At that time, the tea poy had been only recently introduced, and the term was used in its true sense, but it evidently degenerated through

Tea Poy ((caddy-Stand)c.1810

popular ignorance during the Victorian period, as a commentator of 1866 referred in scathing terms to the incorrectness of common contemporary usage. This erroneous usage is unfortunately generally followed at the present day, and the phrase is usually employed to denote what might be better described as a 'tea-chest on stand' or 'caddy-stand', the stand being usually of pillar-and-claw type. Many examples have survived from the Regency period when tea-chests of this kind were first introduced.

Tea Table: any small table intended primarily for the service of tea—but usable for other purposes—including the numerous tripod tables made throughout the Georgian era and the *tipai* ('tea poy') of the early 19th century. Many had galleried tops, some of which consisted of removable trays which constituted the actual tables in accordance with contemporary usage, the remainder of the structures being considered as stands. Some tripod tables had flat, circular tops with notches round the edges to accommodate the legs of large silver salvers. These were described as 'stands', the salvers being called tea (or coffee) tables. Some tea tables with small tops were made in sets, owing to the occasional practice of giving one to each guest. See also China Table.

Tester: a term deriving from old French *teste*, the head, denoting the canopy of a bed. In 15th-century England the canopies of beds were suspended from the ceiling by cords, but from the early 16th century were commonly supported on posts.

Till: a small drawer contained in a larger piece of furniture. This medieval English word is still commonly used to denote a drawer for money in a shop.

Toilet Mirror: although they were known in the middle ages, the earliest surviving English toilet mirrors date from the time of the Restoration, most of the frames being decorated with the relief embroidery called 'stump-work'. These either hung on walls or were supported behind by struts. Later in the reign of Charles II, when the use of silver was spreading over an ever-widening field which sometimes included tables, chairs and even fire-

dogs, the same metal was used for the frames of toilet mirrors which sometimes formed part of elaborate garnitures decorated in the prevailing Netherlandish style. Others might be framed in wood which was often carved and gilt.

Toilet Mirror c.1705

At the end of the 17th century a type was introduced with the mirror pivoted between uprights mounted either on a stand or on a box with drawers and sometimes a miniature bureau, the whole being veneered with walnut or japanned. This variety became especially popular during the reign of Queen Anne. No specific dressing-tables existed at the time, and any convenient side table could be adapted for this purpose by standing a toilet mirror upon it. The box and stand types continued all through the 18th century into the Regency period and beyond, the treatment of the mirror-frames varying according to prevailing fashions. In the Chippendale period, for example, they were sometimes embellished with carved rococo ornament. In the neo-classical phase there was an analogy between the forms of toilet-mirror frames and those of contemporary chair-backs, so that they were shield-shaped or oval, and finally rectangular. Until the late 18th century, the uprights were generally of square-section, but thereafter they were usually turned, the designs becoming increasingly cluttered with annular mouldings. Many other details afford evidence of period: bow-fronts became common in the last quarter of the 18th century as on contemporary chests of drawers, and the brass surrounds of key-holes were often replaced by ivory.

Torchère: see Candle-Stand.

Torus: an architectural term denoting a convex moulding which, in connection with furniture, is usually employed to describe a similar moulding beneath the cornice of a cabinet of the late 17th century, generally forming the front of a shallow drawer.

Towel Horse: also known as a Clothes Horse: references to these objects occurred in the early 18th century but probably none has survived from before about 1790, their fragile construction making them liable to damage. They all consisted of an open arrangement of thin horizontal bars between uprights, but varied in design. The simplest comprised two 'leaves' like the folds of a screen, and would naturally stand up only when the leaves were at an angle to each other. Another kind had a fixed framework with each of the uprights resting on a pair of depressed cabriole legs or horizontal bars with two short feet beneath each. Sometimes an extra leaf was pivoted to each upright and opened like the movable supports of a gate-leg table. From the end of the 18th century the variety resting on transverse bars became especially prevalent, the members being mostly turned. This type continued into the Victorian period with little modification. Nearly all surviving towel-horses are made of mahogany.

Trafalgar Chair: a modern jargon name sometimes used to describe an ordinary Regency chair with 'sabre' legs, often with one of the cross-rails in the back carved to look like a short length of rope. Although the name is invalid, it might be said that it serves as a reminder that the type in question was introduced in about 1805, the year of the Battle of Trafalgar.

Trays: references to trays are found in medieval records where they are described as 'voiders', one of their chief uses being the removal of the débris of a meal. The term was still current as an alternative in the Georgian period. Most sophisticated wooden examples date from after the middle of the 18th century when they began to be made in great variety, mostly of mahogany. Chippendale showed designs for what he described as 'Tea-Trays or Voiders' with fretted

sides, in the 1754 edition of the *Director,* and Hepplewhite, in the *Guide,* illustrated a number of oval examples decorated in precisely the same manner as the tops of contemporary tables, with inlay of various woods in neo-classical designs. During the Regency period wood was largely superseded by japanned metal and papier-mâché as a material for trays. In the late 19th and early 20th centuries, many passable reproductions of late 18th-century oval trays were made, a favourite ornamental motif being a large whelk-shell. These trays are often extremely well-made.

Trestle Table: a table with removable top mounted on trestles. Although fixed or 'dormant' tables were known in the medieval period, it is evident from manuscript illuminations that trestle tables were used even in royal or noble households. They remained in general use until the early 16th century.

Tridarn: a name given in Wales to a press cupboard or hall cupboard in three stages, the topmost being usually open and surmounted by a canopy. The type is not exclusively Welsh, and was made in other parts in the 17th century, usually of oak.

Tripod Table: See Pedestal Table.

Truckle Bed, also known as a Trundle Bed: a low bed, with a wheel on each leg, which could be moved easily or pushed under a main bed when not in use, current from the late 15th century until about 1740.

Trussing Bed: trussing beds could be dismantled and folded up for travelling, and were in use from the 14th to the 16th century. Their construction must remain a matter of conjecture, but it is possible that the bedstock was furnished with hinges at the corners, as in the case of certain 16th-century table-frames.

Trussing Coffer: a chest of moderate size used for travelling from the late middle ages to the 17th century. Attempts have been made from time to time to distinguish between the terms 'chest' and 'coffer', but in practice they were interchangeable. Some trussing coffers had lids which were either canted or shaped like part of a cylinder, and they

might also be covered with leather and have an iron loop-handle at each end.

Tulip Wood: a hard, striped wood of a brownish yellow colour sometimes tinged with red. It was imported into England from Brazil from about 1760, and was used almost entirely for veneers, especially in the form of cross-banding. It is usually found only on the more expensive furniture of the second half of the 18th century.

Tunbridge Ware: a decorative wood ware made in Tunbridge Wells, Kent, from the middle of the 17th century and elsewhere in the 18th century, consisting mostly of games boards, boxes, etc., embellished with veneered patterns, chiefly geometrical, in contrasting natural colours. Occasionally, the designs were of a pictorial character. A noticeably popular border design was in the form of counterchanged sharp triangles.

Twist Turning: spiral turning on the legs of furniture was used sparsely just after the middle of the 17th century, but became especially prevalent after 1660, when the monarchy was restored and many Continental fashions were introduced. In England, twist turning often differed from its European equivalent in that the spaces between the ridges were wider: on the Continent, these ridges tended to be larger and closer together, so that the effect was rather like loosely-twisted rope. On chairs, twist turning declined in incidence in about 1685 and was replaced by balusters and similar forms, but continued to be used on tables at least until the end of the 17th century. In the provinces, of course, the fashion lingered on, and the banisters of mahogany staircases sometimes took this form in the first half of the 18th century. Basically, twist turning was a more strongly-emphasised version of a type of renaissance architectural column.

V

Varnish: varnish made of linseed, nut or poppy oil was probably used on some English oak furniture, as an alternative to polychrome painting, soon after these oils began to be employed as media for the painting of pictures in the first half of the 15th century. Many surviving pieces of furniture of the 16th and 17th centuries owe their dark tone, and probably their preservation, to the fact that they were covered with oil varnish as soon as they were made. In the second half of the 17th century, spirit varnish, consisting of Oriental shell or seed lac dissolved in alcohol, began to be used instead of oil varnish on decorative furniture, especially that of a Chinese character, but this kind of surface treatment must not be confused with polishing. Oil and beeswax continued to be used for this purpose until after 1820. See French Polish.

Veneer: thin layers of wood, at first hand-sawn, applied to the surface of a piece of furniture, by means of an adhesive. Though used to some extent on oak furniture of the Elizabethan and Jacobean periods in a decorative manner, the practice of veneering the whole or major part of a carcase did not begin until after the Restoration in 1660. The wood chiefly employed for the purpose was then walnut, but mahogany and other woods were increasingly used from about 1725. In the late 18th century satinwood enjoyed a considerable vogue, but rosewood was generally preferred after 1800. Some early veneers were as much as an eighth of an inch thick, but they became thinner with the passage of time.

Verre Eglomisé: the decoration of glass by painting on the reverse side and backing it with metal foils including gold and silver. The name derives, without good reason, from that of Jean Baptiste Glomy, a Parisian collector and framer who died shortly before the outbreak of the French Revolution, though the technique had been practised in the Levant many centuries before and had been popular in Italy during the renaissance. It was also employed in England in the second half of the 16th century in association with goldsmiths' work, and some monumental salts, treated in this manner, have survived from the Elizabethan period. It was especially frequent on the crests of mirror-frames in the late 18th and early 19th centuries.

Vile, William (*d.* **1767**): partner of John Cobb and the most distinguished London cabinet-maker for over two decades from about 1740. He worked for the Prince of Wales, who continued to employ him after his accession as George III in 1760. His style, in both the late baroque and rococo tastes, was sumptuous and monumental, while the craftsmanship evinced in construction and finish was unexcelled. Although he did not enjoy the same degree of publicity which Chippendale re-

ceived as a result of the publication of the *Director* it is evident, from surviving examples attributed to him, that his cabinet-work was greatly superior.

Vitruvian Scroll: running ornament of classical origin, deriving its name from that of the Roman architect and engineer Vitruvius, who published, in the reign of Augustus, an important work entitled *De*

Vitruvian Scroll

Architectura in which this ornament was illustrated. It consists of connected scrolls shaped like a series of waves with curling crests. It occurred on English furniture in the early 18th century and again in the neo-classical phase in the second half of the century. It was carried out in various ways including carving, painting, inlaying and the application of ormolu.

W

Wainscot: originally signified any sort of wood, shipped from Baltic ports, suitable for wains or wagons, but in the 17th century came to mean timber for panelling or furniture, usually oak. See Oak.

Walnut: a small amount of English walnut was used occasionally for furniture from the earliest times, but the trees take a long time to mature in the English climate and were, in any event, grown for their fruit rather than their timber. Walnut succeeded oak as the fashionable wood for furniture effectively from about 1660, and although rather more English walnut was used than is generally supposed, supplies came chiefly from Savoie and the English colony of Virginia. The latter was known as 'black walnut' on account of the dark streaks in the grain, and was considered the better of the two varieties, though French walnut from Savoie was also highly esteemed by English cabinet-makers. John Evelyn, the famous 17th-century diarist, records that walnut was sometimes subjected to mild heat in a kiln and then polished with the oil which it exuded. It was widely used in the form of veneer on case furniture and in the solid for legs, etc., but was gradually replaced by mahogany from about 1720 onwards and had been almost completely abandoned by the middle of the century.

Wardrobe: see Clothes-Press.

Wave-Crest Ornament: a descriptive term for Vitruvian scrolls (*q.v.*).

Wedgwood, Josiah (1730–1795): some time after the establishment of his celebrated pottery at Etruria (1769), Wedgwood supplied ceramic plaques of classical design to cabinet-makers to be inset into pieces of furniture. This form of embellishment was not used to any great extent, but has survived on a few painted commodes and other pieces from the late 18th century. The technique was more prevalent in France in the reign of Louis XVI and this was no doubt the source of inspiration of the English version. When used excessively the effect is incongruous.

Wellington Chest: a tall, narrow chest of shallow drawers, first occurring in the early 19th century, secured by locking a hinged flap attached to one edge, running from top to bottom and slightly overlapping the drawers.

Welsh Dresser: a misleading term applied to a dresser with drawers, surmounted by shelves sometimes having small spice-cupboards contrived in the side supports. The type was introduced from the Netherlands in the 17th century and survived in the British Isles until the end of the 18th century. The alternative term 'Dutch Dresser' is more accurate.

What-Not: a movable stand of varying height consisting of four turned supports with usually rectangular shelves between them arranged in tiers. The what-not was in existence before 1800 but was apparently

not described by this name until after 1805. Regency examples were made of either rosewood or mahogany, and a few embodied shallow drawers at the base.

Wig-Stand: wig-stands, or peruke-blocks, must have been in use soon after the fashion for wearing periwigs was introduced from France by Charles

Wig-Stand

II in 1660, but the earliest surviving specimens date from the first half of the 18th century. Nearly all were somewhat after the fashion of a wooden candlestick, with a circular base and a vertical shaft surmounted by a round pad, but a few supported blocks shaped like human heads without features. They were stood on tables or some other convenient surface and were seldom more than 18 in. high. They ceased to be made soon after 1760 when wigs began to go out of fashion. See also Bason Stand.

Window Stool: a long, upholstered stool designed to be placed by a window, varying in length according to the space to be filled but commonly about the size of two chairs.

Window Stool
(Hepplewhite)

Window stools were similar to other long stools in being open along the back, but differed in having ends like low chairbacks. In this specific form they first appeared in the middle of the 18th century, when they were sometimes carved with rococo ornament, but were made in greater numbers in the neo-classical period at a time when the incidence of ordinary stools was declining. Hepplewhite illustrated many designs for window stools in the *Guide*.

Windsor Chair: an all-wood chair, introduced in the early 18th century and still made, with a back comprising chiefly vertical turned sticks or spindles enclosed within a hoop or surmounted by a cresting-rail giving the appearance of a comb. The legs are mostly turned, though the front legs of some examples of the Chippendale period were of cabriole form. No attempt seems to have been made at this time to include any rococo features as on other furniture, but a number were made whose backs displayed a strong Gothic influence. In these and other types some or all of the spindles were replaced by pierced splats. Nearly all parts were fitted

Windsor Chair, c.1750

together by dowelling. Seats have almost invariably been made of elm, the hoops and arms of yew and the legs and spindles of beech, though mahogany was used to a small extent in the 18th century for certain details. In the Georgian era, Windsor chairs were often used in gardens, those intended for this purpose being generally painted green.

Wine Cooler: tubs of metal or other materials containing cold water in which flasks of wine

were immersed before and during meals were in use as early as the 15th century, and silver specimens have survived from the 17th and 18th centuries, but elegant wooden examples lined with lead appear to have been introduced soon after mahogany became fashionable. Their stylistic evolution was analogous with that of other furniture though the actual receptacles generally remained of oval shape. Early types, for example, were mounted on short cabriole legs with claw-and-ball or paw feet. These were followed by the various kinds of legs and other details current during the Chippendale, Adam and Regency periods. In the last quarter of the 18th century a common version was of plain mahogany encircled by two polished brass hoops, and in the early 19th century a type shaped like a sarcophagus was especially popular. The ice used with these coolers was collected during the winter and stored in subterranean ice-houses so that a supply was available throughout the year. They are often indistinguishable from cellarets (*q.v.*).

Wine Table: various kinds of special tables connected with drinking were devised in the late 18th century, some of them persisting into the Regency period. One type was in the form of a tripod table of normal proportions, with notches round the edge in which glasses were hung bowl-downwards, while a large area of the top, enclosed by a gallery, had a platform pierced with circular holes of varying size for glasses and decanters. Other designs existed at the same time including one by Hepplewhite, published seven years after his death, entitled 'A Gentleman's Social Table', a feature common to all being the open or covered recesses for decanters and glasses. In the early 19th century the most popular wine table was of a narrow horseshoe shape, with metal coasters for the decanters sliding in a trough or hinged to a brass rod.

It should be noted that all these tables were of normal height. The modern low, reproduction tripod tables with small tops, usually called wine tables, are, in fact, descendants of the kettle-stands of the first half of the 18th century.

Wing Chair: a kind of upholstered easy chair introduced in about 1680, one of the earliest versions being known as a 'sleeping chayre' and having a back which could be let down on a ratchet to allow the occupant to doze in comfort. Wings ('cheeks') were either parallel-sided or of the more familiar ogee shape, the latter being more usual. Cabriole legs appeared shortly before 1700 and stretchers were always present in the underframes until after 1710. The type continued into the second half of the 18th century, gradually declining in

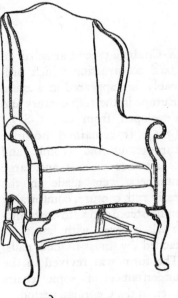

Wing Chair, c.1700

incidence, the legs reflecting all the usual changes in fashion. The most elegant and well-proportioned examples were made in the early 18th century.

Work Table: a small table for needlework occurring in great variety from about 1760 onwards. The type was especially popular in the late 18th century when it was made of either mahogany or satinwood and commonly contained recep-tacles for reels, bobbins, etc., and a pendant silk bag. One variety had a raised rim to the top and shelves beneath. In the early 19th century, the work table, sometimes veneered with rosewood, was often supported on a central pillar instead of four legs as previously: a feature frequently found on other pieces of furniture of the same period. Rare examples were equipped with chess or backgammon boards.

X

X-Chair: a type of armchair of fixed construction which probably first appeared in western Europe in the 14th century and developed from the X-Stool (*q.v.*). It remained popular throughout the Gothic and renaissance periods and large numbers were made in the early 17th century, comfortably upholstered and with the framework covered with fabric attached by brass-headed nails. The form was revived in the underframes of some chairs even in the Georgian period.

X-Stool: a common form of medieval stool with two sets of X-shaped supports originally pivoted at the points of intersection like scissors to enable it

X- Stool, 14th. Century

to be folded. The type was of immense antiquity and was used in ancient Egypt, Greece and Rome. In the 16th century it was evidently considered no longer necessary for such stools to be folded up, and thereafter they were almost invariably fixed. The form survived into the 19th century, examples being often carved and gilded.

Y

Yew: English yew trees yield a hard, springy timber which, when polished, often has a surface as close as that of horn. It was used for inlay in the 16th and 17th centuries and very occasionally in the solid. After the Restoration (1660) it was sometimes employed as veneer, and oyster pieces (*q.v.*) cut from the branches provided an alternative to the more usual laburnum, walnut and olive until the early 18th century. At the latter period, burr-yew was sometimes applied to case-furniture. Parts of Windsor chairs (*q.v.*) were often made of yew throughout the 18th century.

Z

Zebra Wood: a hard South American timber, light in tone with emphatic dark brown streaks. It was employed for cross-banding and sometimes normal veneer in the late 18th and early 19th centuries but apparently became unobtainable after about 1820, so that examples are rare.

SELECTED BIBLIOGRAPHY

Cescinsky, Herbert and Gribble, Ernest, *Early English Furniture and Woodwork*.

Edwards, Ralph, *The Dictionary of English Furniture* (3 vols.), *Hepplewhite Furniture Designs, Sheraton Furniture Designs*.

Fastnedge, Ralph, *English Furniture Styles 1500–1830*

Hughes, Therle, *Old English Furniture*.

Macdonald-Taylor, Margaret, *English Furniture*.

Musgrave, Clifford, *Regency Furniture, Furniture of the Adam Period*.

Roe, Fred, *A History of Oak Furniture*.

Symonds, R. W., *Chippendale Furniture Designs*.